AF559661

CAPITAL ACCOUNT CONVERTIBILITY IN INDIA

Contents

Preface

The Bengal Economic Association (BEA) since 1995 has published so far nine books edited by economists of eminence like Prof. Dhires Bhattacharyya, Prof. P.R. Brahmananda, Prof. Alak Ghosh, Prof. Raj Kumar Sen, etc., mostly in honour of distinguished economists of the country. This book is its Tenth venture to cater economic ideas on Capital Account Convertibility in India written by reputed economists of the country as well as young scholars.

The present volume with the title "Capital Account Convertibility in India" is an attempt to capture the various aspects of this hotly debated issue hovering over the country since the initiation of the Tarapore Committee during the latter half of the 1990s, which defines the concept as the 'freedom to convert local financial assets into foreign financial assets and vice versa at market determined rates of exchange' and laid down fiscal consolidation, a mandated inflation target, and strengthening of the financial system as its three main preconditions. However, full capital account convertibility, which allows domestic residence to acquire foreign assets, also absorbs reserves, but it raises the risk of capital outflows and crisis unless markets and institutions are well developed. Therefore economists are unanimous that it has to be introduced gradually and in a correct sequence. It is in this context that this volume covers both theoretical and empirical aspects of the issue as well as expands further the frontier of the growing literature on the theme, importance of which is increasing in recent times. This book contains a set of 11 selected articles including the keynote paper by D. M. Nachane presented in the 27th Annual Conference of the Bengal Economic Association held at Lady Brabourne College,

Kolkata. Following the precedence of the publication of the proceedings of its earlier seminars, conferences, etc., the BEA decided to publish this volume as a part of its academic activities and to circulate widely the issues and conclusions derived in that conference among the academic fraternities at large. We hope that this edited volume will not only provide good reading material on "Capital Account Convertibility in India" but also help the students, teachers and researchers of economic science for a better understanding of the issue, and will help the government and policy-makers to take better decisions in the present economic environment. The major contribution of these articles is available in a summarized form from the Introduction which follows.

We are thankful to the contributors, without whose co-operation this volume could not be published in time. Last but not the least, we thank Shri G.S. Bhatia of Deep & Deep Publications Pvt. Ltd., New Delhi for his co-operation and help to publish this in an elegant manner.

Kolkata

BISWAJIT CHATTERJEE
ASIM K. KARMAKAR
Editors

List of Contributors

DR. D.M. NACHANE
Director, IGIDR, Mumbai.

DR. SMRITI MUKHERJEE
Former Reader, Gokhale Institute of Politics and Economics, Pune.

BISWAJIT CHATTERJEE
Professor of Economics and Dean, Faculty of Arts, Jadavpur University, Kolkata.
and President, Bengal Economic Association.

DR. RAM PRATAP SINHA
Reader in Economics, Government College of Engineering and Leather Technology, Kolkata.

DR. DHIRAJ KUMAR BANDYOPADHYAY
Research Associate in Economics, CUES, University of Calcutta.

DR. JAYDEB SARKHEL
Professor of Economics, Department of Commerce, Burdwan University, West Bengal.

CHANCHAL CHATTERJEE
UGC Project Fellow, Commerce Department, Burdwan University, West Bengal.

GAGARI CHAKRABARTI
Lecturer, Department of Economics, Presidency College, Kolkata.

DR. ASIM K. KARMAKAR
Senior Lecturer, Department of Economics, Jadavpur University, Kolkata.

DEBESH BHOWMIK

Member, IIDS, Kolkata.

DR. DEBENDRA KUMAR DAS

Professor of Economics, BRA Bihar University, Muzaffarpur, Bihar.

SANKHANATH BANDYOPADHYAY

Research Associate, ICFAI Research Centre, Kolkata.

DR. PUSHPA TARAFDAR

Former Reader in Economics, Sarojini Naidu College for Women, Kolkata.

SAIKAT BHATTACHARYYA

Assistant Teacher, Bangabasi College- School, Kolkata.

Introduction

The issue of introducing convertibility in the capital account of the Indian economy has been debated in the policy circles in the context of liberalization of our economy and following the recommendations of the Tarapore Committee successive governments at the Centre has toyed with possibility of liberalizing the country's capital account by introducing Capital Account Convertibility (CAC). The present book is an outgrowth of the conference organized by the Bengal Economic Association in 2007 on this theme where different scholars have focused on the merits as well as difficulties associated with such a policy move. The present book consists of eleven research papers where the authors have endeavoured to analyse the pros and cons of CAC and to identify whether the time is ripe for India to move to full CAC convertibility in our country.

The theme paper of the book is written by Professor D.M. Nachane, who has discussed the arguments for and against capital account convertibility (CAC) in India. The paper explores theoretically the impact of CAC on financial stability, outlines its macroeconomic effects on the real economy and delineates the state of CAC liberalization in India. The paper also considers measures for coping with capital inflows (mainly short-term flows) that can have pronounced impacts on output, growth and fiscal budget, principally on its capital investment component—the effects being transmitted through exchange rate variation via the cost of external debt servicing and also through domestic interest rate. The author has also enlightened the definition of CAC, types, measures, New Classical *Vs.* Keynesian view of financial markets linked with CAC, IMF advocacy, virtuous debt cycle, critique of the IMF model, the second Tarapore Committee's recommendations as well as several risks and important distortions associated with capital account liberalization (CAL) in our country. The paper argues that several of the theoretical claims underlying the CAC policy are flawed and that the empirical case is not reassuring either. The major findings of this papers are that capital account openness is not growth-enhancing and if there is growth, it is only for relatively high-income countries, and only if such growth is accompanied by prudential safeguards measures that one can argue for the introduction of CAC. In the Indian context, the author strongly argues that the time is not ripe to go in for full CAC in that full CAC promises no large benefits, while it increases the risk of things going wrong. Secondly, Professor Nachane has cast doubt about the activity of two committees (especially Tarapore II) arguing that perhaps the committee has not gone into the detailed examination of all the risks attached to CAC. This may invite a great danger for a country like India.

The paper by Biswajit Chatterjee and Ram Pratap Sinha has argued that the euphoria on capital account liberalization is short-lived as the emerging market economics in the 1990s and beyond have had the experience of severe banking and currency crisis. In this backdrop, the paper makes a survey of the capital account liberalization process in India and examines the possible dangerous consequences of India's opening up of the capital account since 1997 and macroeconomic implications of CAC as it is often found that CAC has facilitated the recurrence of financial sectors crisis in the emerging market economics including India. The authors have raised a very pertinent question: Will India be able to insulate its capital market from negative shocks in future when FII will be much more significant?

Smriti Mukherjee has examined basically two issues viz. how the accumulation of foreign exchange reserves after the CAL is to be utilized, and whether higher macroeconomic volatility following CAC as has occurred in several countries is applicable to India. She, however, has discussed the issues of CAC that arose in the wake of debt crisis of 1980s where higher weightage was given to private capital flows in the light of the current international scenario with a theoretical perspective.

Asim K. Karmakar, in his paper has presented the conceptual issues regarding CAC and has discussed the CAC debate in India. According to him, the Indian resident will be able to use the world capital market for risk diversification and maximize the return on their resources. He has also pointed out how Indian economy has moved from exchange control to convertibility. He has suggested that CAC in India requires several prerequisites in terms of strong macroeconomic policy framework and soundness and efficiency of financial systems and markets, which are still lacking in the Indian economy.

Dhiraj Kumar Bandyopadhyay has suggested that for reasonably long periods of time and specially in recent years, there has been a reverse net transfer of financial resources from LDCs to rich countries. Most episodes of inter-related banking and currency crises in emerging markets have been preceded by financial liberalization and increased access to foreign capital markets. At the end, he has argued that the full capital account convertibility as well as liberalization is at least, in the perspective of world financial system, about 10 to 15 years premature in LDCs.

In fact, there are several issues associated with CAC such as the benefits expected from CAC, its significant impact on different sectors of the economy like Banks and Financial Institutions, Stock Exchange, Exchange Rates, etc., and the preconditions to be fulfilled or the precautions to be taken before going in for full capital mobility as well as international experience with a free capital mobility. These issues have been attempted in the paper by Jaydeb Sarkhel and Chanchal Chatterjee.

Gagari Chakrabarti has raised the issue of riskiness associated with full CAC in India She has divided her paper on four parts as—Benefits of CAC for developing countries, international experience with CAC, lessons from past experience, when CAC is possible and CAC in India. From her analysis, it is found that presence of distortions due to non-information might lead to reverse capital flight with CAC and issue of speedy sequencing of the liberalization process are important in a casino economy. To reap full advantage of CAC, domestic financial sector reforms and corporate financial structure reforms to cope with capital inflow and outflow are vital for India.

In their joint paper Debesh Bhowmik and Debendra Kumar Das have started with the meaning of capital account convertibility and have extended their analysis towards rupee convertibility, long-run exchange rate mechanism and balance of payments, and matters related to Tarapore Committee recommendations on CAC in India. In the paper, they have argued that the implementation of full convertibility of Rupee is not a new concept to Indian economy in the sense of globalization. The rupee convertibility was a deferred, delegalised, delocalized and therefore a divitalized kind of convertibility. The paper has ended with the view that the success of full convertibility of Rupee depends on the degree of achievement on monetary integration and financial integration in the global market and also depends on how far Indian currency system can link with international monetary system.

Sankhanath Bandyopadhyay has highlighted some of the most important factors helping India to maintain surplus in the BOP. He has tried to identify them and analyse the extent they are reliable in order to maintain the external viability of the Indian economy. Moreover, some specific issues related to the monetary and fiscal policies and corporate debt market, which are sensitive to the aspect of full Capital Account Convertibility (CAC), are also discussed by the author.

In the context of the hefty accumulation of dollar assets and the growing current account surplus by India and many East Asian Countries like China, Taiwan, Japan and Korea as a by-product of a strategy of export-led growth, the paper by Pushpa Tarafdar examines the issue of CAC and CAL both of which is largely driven by globalization of financial flows. Also her paper deals with the behaviour of capital flows in the 1990s in the emerging economies and its impact on exchange rate movements. The conclusion of the paper is that mere CAC may be conducive to growth but actual performance of the economy crucially depends on host of factors including sound macroeconomic policies and strong domestic financial system.

The last paper in this volume is by Saikat Bhattacharyya. In his paper, Bhattacharyya has built up a model on rational expectation and has developed an analytical framework to show where the opening up of capital account enhances any additional volatility into the domestic stock market. This has been shown in the light of the broad perspective of Rational Expectation Hypothesis. After using rational expectation based 'Dividend Discount Model' of stock price determination and solving it through recursive method, he ultimately shows the effect of CAL on the stock market of the emerging market economies. At this, he finds two alternative sets of solutions, one of which accepts the speculative bubble that creates price risk and exposes the stock market to the speculators. With full convertible capital account, this may put the domestic economy into deep trouble, he argues. He has also suggested some policies to demolish the bubbles that occur during the capital account liberalization process.

The present collection, it is hoped, will throw new lights to the debate on CAC, and would be an important addition to the existing literature on the subject. It is expected to provide some guidelines for the formulation of appropriate policies in future in this regard. We thank all contributors for their kind contribution and to Shri G.S. Bhatia for publishing the book in an elegant manner.

Kolkata

BISWAJIT CHATTERJEE
ASIM K. KARMAKAR

1

Capital Account Convertibility in India: Revisiting the Debate

D.M. NACHANE

ABSTRACT

Capital account liberalization (CAL) is an example of "orchestrated harmonisation" of policy advice emanating from academic institutions, think tanks and multilateral institutions in the developed world, which seek to push the doctrines of new classical economics. Capital account liberalization is one such policy advice. This paper examines the theoretical case for CAL and finds that it is subject to important caveats relating to moral hazard, asymmetric information and agency problems. CAL has proved occasionally beneficial but only for relatively developed countries and only if accompanied by appropriate prudential measures. The line taken by several apologists for CAL that the risks of financial instability are negligible and hence more than compensated by the benefits, ignores the magnitude of the potential costs of a crisis.

I. INTRODUCTION

It is undeniable that in the last three decades,

cataclysmic changes have been underway in the functioning and organization of the world economy. Following Went (2002-03), three changes may be singled out for special attention:

(i) A phenomenal increase in the number of global markets for products and services (especially financial services).
(ii) A growing role for "footloose" multinationals (a term owing to Reich (1992)) in the global economy.
(iii) An enhanced role for supranational organizations (G-8, IMF, BIS, WTO, OECD, etc.) and regional associations (EU, NAFTA, ASEAN, etc.), with a commensurate emasculation of the role of nation states.

While these developments are well recognized, a related phenomenon seems to have attracted relatively little attention, viz. the unchallenged sway that the doctrines of new-classical economics[1] and monetarism have acquired over the policy advice emanating from academic institutions, international "think tanks" and multilateral institutions. This mould of thinking translates into policy recipes such as export-oriented growth, privatization, deregulation, etc. and are religiously followed by many EMEs and LDCs, (under "persuasion" from international organizations) with no attention to local conditions. The actual results of such policies are often mixed, and though the success stories are inevitably highlighted, failures tend to get under-reported and attributed to faulty implementation rather than the flawed advice in the first place.

Capital account convertibility (henceforth CAC for short) is one such instance of "orchestrated harmonization", and will form the subject matter of this paper.

2. CAC AND FINANCIAL INSTABILITY

2.1 Short-term and Long-term Capital Flows

Many advocates of the reforms process in India tend to

view CAC as the last bastion to overcome in India's triumphal march towards globalization. To all such it may come as a surprise that much of the post-World War II period (the so-called "golden age of capitalism") was an era of heavily regulated capital flows in the Western economies. Indeed the founding fathers of the Bretton Woods system recognized the incompatibility of a free trade and stable exchange rate regime with free capital mobility. Indeed, Keynes describes proposals *"to stabilize exchange rates and promote free trade without limiting international capital mobility" as "exercises in squaring the circle"* (see Felix (1995)). Reflecting the Keynesian orthodoxy then prevalent, the IMF Executive board in 1956 reaffirmed the right of member countries to impose capital controls. With the breakdown of the Bretton Woods system in the 1970s and under the powerful impact of Milton Friedman's writings (and later the emergence of the New Classical Economics School), the intellectual climate became less propitious towards capital controls, with the general policy sentiment veering to the view that *"no country can share in the benefits of international trade unless it allows capital to move freely enough to finance that trade, and modern financial markets are sophisticated and open enough that capital transactions can no longer be compartmentalized as trade-related or speculative"* (*Boughton* (1997)). Reflecting the new thinking, the IMF's Internal Committee in April 1997 unanimously voted in favour of amending the Articles of the Fund to allow capital controls only as emergency measures in exceptional situations.

To avoid a possible confusion, it is best at the outset to clarify that there are two levels of debates about the desirability of capital flows and for analytical convenience, it is best to keep them separate. The more prominent debate currently is about short-term capital flows and this is what we will be focusing on here. This is not pronouncedly ideological, with opponents of capital inflows being on both sides of the political spectrum (one irritating stratagem commonly employed by CAC advocates is to dub all opponents of CAC as "leftists" if not "Marxists"). There is also, however, an older debate about the desirability of long-term capital flows with distinct ideological overtones. The intellectual advocacy of long-term capital flows is normally based on some variant of the IMF's Financial Programming model (*Khan and Haque* (1990), with capital inflows into EMEs (Emerging Market Economies) viewed as raising domestic investment rates over the domestic savings rate, dampening the effects of exogenous shocks and promoting efficiency in EMEs via transfer of technology and financial skills (see also *Eichengreen* (1996) for a more nuanced expression of this viewpoint). This view has been challenged in predominantly leftist intellectual circles (see e.g. *Plender* (1997), *Robinson* (1996), *Chesnais* (1994), *Went* (2000), etc.) as imperialism masquerading in the guise of neo-liberalism. Recently, Singh (2002) in a detailed empirical study finds that unregulated FDI may do more harm than good, and where FDI has been least regulated it has also been least beneficial, while Rakshit (2001) argues that the theoretical conditions for the postulated benefits of FDI to be realized are rather restrictive. While CAC connotes liberalization of both long-term and short-term capital flows, it is important to bear in mind that the issues raised for the two types of flows are fundamentally different. Stiglitz (2000) for example, while emphatically regarding short-term capital flows as disruptive, finds *"the argument for foreign direct investment compelling"*. The issues raised by long-term capital flows, though important, are too vast to be encompassed within the scope of a single article and are therefore not dealt with here. Our focus for the purposes of this paper remains the various issues raised by the inflows/ outflows of short-term capital.

2.2 New-Classical Versus Keynesian View of Financial Markets

The New Classical case for free (short-term) capital mobility rests on the so-called *efficient markets doctrine*. As is well known this hypothesis posits that current market prices of financial assets embody rationally all the known information about prospective returns from the asset. Future uncertainty is of the *"white noise"* kind and *"noise traders"* (speculators) may succeed in pushing the markets temporarily away from equilibrium. But with market clearing continuously, *"rational traders"* will bring the system back to equilibrium, by taking countervailing positions, and imposing heavy losses on those speculators who bet against the fundamentals. Equilibrium asset prices will therefore be altered only when there are *"shocks"* to the fundamentals, and while supply shocks are inevitable, the severity of demand shocks can be tempered by policy aimed at giving more access to information about fundamentals to market participants, and avoiding *"policy surprises"* or attempts to control asset prices. Such a view underpins the *"tough love"* approach of the IMF to dealing with currency crises—an approach which is fundamentally skewed in that international credit banks who usually precipitate such crises by their indiscriminate lending, rolling over of credit and tax avoidance strategies are seen in the role of victims, whereas the major blame is apportioned to the crisis-affected countries for their bungled macroeconomic management (current account deficits, overvalued exchange rates, loose monetary policy, etc.) and for "misleading" investors by withholding key information about fundamentals. Such governments are then administered "bail out" packages with strong attached conditionalities as part of the "tough love" treatment. The post-crisis sternness contrasts markedly with the pre-crisis exhortations of top IMF officials as well as Treasury representatives of the US and European powers, to EME and LDC governments about the desirability of private capital inflows. For example, the Robichek-Lawson doctrine (so-called after Walter Robichek, Director of Western Hemisphere operations of the IMF in the 1980s and Tony Lawson, Chancellor of the Exchequer under Margaret Thatcher) for example, regards the financing of rising current account deficits with increasing private foreign liabilities as a matter of little concern, maintaining that countries that pursued free market policies and fiscal restraint, could always cover current account deficits with capital account inflows from global financial markets. Diaz-Alexandro (1985), Devlin (1989) and Felix (1998) attribute the Latin American crises of the 1980s to the uncritical acceptance of this advice by several countries in that region.

The new classical orthodoxy about free capital mobility is crucially contingent on the EMH (efficient market hypothesis). Actual trading strategies of forex traders are in systematic violation of rational market behaviour. *"I'd be a bum in the street with a tin cup if the markets were efficient"* is a famous remark by none other than Warren Buffet. Theories of human decision-making (see *Kahneman and Tversky* (1984), *Rabin and Thaler* (2001), etc.) argue that in the face of complex uncertain situations, individuals do not proceed via maximizing expected utility but using *cognitive heuristics*. Such heuristics is an aid to reducing a complex task to a manageable proportion but often introduces systematic biases. The bulk of the econometric evidence on financial markets is also contra the EMH. (see e.g. *Shiller* (1981), *LeRoy and Porter* (1981), *Shleifer and Summers* (1990), etc.).

Increasingly economists are realizing that the 1930s Keynesian description of financial markets as being *"casinos"* guided by *"herd instincts"* is nearer the mark (than the EMH) as a description of how real world forex markets operate today (see e.g. *Russel and Torbey* (2002), *Huberman and Regev* (2001), etc.). In the Keynesian view, investors in financial assets are not interested in a long-term perspective, but rather in speculating on short-run price behaviour. This is specially true in forex markets where day trading is the rule rather than the exception. Far from basing their expectations on prospective behaviour of the underlying fundamentals, such investors are more likely to base their opinions on market sentiments (i.e. the opinion of the other members of their group). This lends a dangerous edge of volatility to financial markets as any "news" if it affects market sentiment strongly (in either direction) is likely to produce mood swings in market sentiment, even if the "news" in question is unlikely to alter long-term fundamentals. If one accepts the Keynesian view of asset price behaviour, then the case for CAC virtually collapses as the damage that unregulated capital flows can impose on an economy become apparent. Volatile capital flows can produce violent swings in important asset prices such as real estate, equities and of course the exchange rate itself, especially if they are pro-cyclical as noted by Williamson and Drabek (1998), Singh (2002), etc. The fragility of the financial system is also enhanced by freer capital mobility. In two important recent studies viz. *Kaminsky and Reinhart* (1999) and *Demirguc-Kunt and Detragiache* (1998), the link between financial liberalization, exchange rate crises and banking crises is clearly brought out. Demirguc-Kunt and Detragiache (1998), for example, argue that financial liberalization intensifies competition among banks, who in their eagerness to preserve market shares could indulge in indiscriminate and risky credit operations (moral hazard problem). During bullish periods, debt leveraging can augment the expected return from financial position-taking by corporate borrowers. Wider asset price movements also erode the ability of banks and other financial institutions to adequately collateralize their loans, while competition restrains them from raising the risk premia on loans. Thus in a regime of capital account liberalization, with adequate prudential banking norms not in place, currency crises can easily translate into more general financial crises.

Thus the theoretical case for CAC seems on rather weak grounds. The position is aptly summed up by Stiglitz (2000) *"it is certainly clear now that the position (of the IMF) was maintained either as a matter of ideology or of special interests, and not on the basis of careful analysis of theory, historical experience or a wealth of econometric studies. Indeed, it has become increasingly clear that there is not only no case for capital market (account ?) liberalization but that there is a fairly compelling case against full liberalization" (parentheses mine).*

2.3 Risks of Capital Account Liberalization

Let us now examine more closely the types of risks attendant on a capital account liberalization programme. Broadly speaking, these risks may be classified into five categories: (i) Currency Risk, (ii) Capital Flight Risk, (iii) Fragility Risk, (iv) Contagion risk, and (v) Sovereignty Risk. Each of these risks we now discuss in some detail.

Currency Risk

This refers to the possibility of a sudden precipitous devaluation of a country's currency. The risk is particularly pronounced for EMEs embarking on an ambitious programme of capital account liberalization without adequate safeguards in place. In such countries reserves may be insufficient to cover significant episodes of investor exit, and additionally, their ability to manage multilateral currency rescue operations might be limited.

Capital Flight Risk

This occurs when non-resident holders of liquid financial assets sell-off their holdings *en masse*. The reasons for the herd-like behaviour of foreign investors run along the lines discussed in Section 2.2. But two factors act as further aggravating factors. Firstly, investor herd behaviour is very frequently an outcome of the safety in numbers syndrome brought on by a shared lack of trust in the reliability of macroeconomic information emerging from EMEs. Secondly, foreign investors often tend to assess the risks in terms of a region as a whole, failing to distinguish between different EMEs within the same region. This makes EMEs vulnerable to bouts of general capital flight.

Fragility Risk

Fragility refers to the vulnerability of the borrowers (corporates and banks) to internal or external shocks. Basically such fragility can be traced to three sources:

Maturity mismatch (i.e. financing long-term obligations with short-term credit)

(i) Foreign currency denominated debts which are subject to changes in value under a freely floating exchange rate
(ii) Non-transparent . . . overborrowing/overinvesting made possible by the growing derivates and futures markets.

Sovereignty Risk

This type of risk pertains to the constraints that a domestic government may face in its ability to pursue independent national policies in the event of a crisis. Such constraints could arise on various counts—

(i) Foreign governments and multilateral institutions may force contractionary policies on the domestic government to stem capital flight.

(ii) Investors may also be reluctant to return (following a crisis) unless explicit government guarantees are available on monetary, trade or fiscal policy (or sometimes even on policies specific to certain sectors such as telecommunications, oil extraction, etc.)

(iii) Global financial integration also implies that in general the ability of small open economies to pursue counter-cyclical policies may be impaired if their business cycles are out of sync with the business cycles of major economies. In particular, the difficulties confronting monetary policy formulation are compounded manifold (see Section 2.4 below).

Contagion Risk

Finally, contagion risk refers to the possibility of a country coming under a crisis threat following a crisis in an other economy, with which its trade, investment and finance are closely interlinked.

2.4 Capital Flows and Monetary Policy

Capital inflows create several special problems for the conduct of monetary policy. As a matter of fact, a famous *trilemma* succinctly sums up the various issues involved. The *trilemma* in question (see *Bernanke* (2005) for a recent exposition) refers to the impossibility of maintaining in simultaneous operation (for a given country) all three of the following policy regimes: (i) an open capital account, (ii) a fixed exchange rate, and (iii) an independent domestic monetary policy. Of course, in practice, concepts like "openness", "fixity" or "independence" are not absolute, but relative or even fuzzy. Hence the *trilemma* needs to be interpreted as a move in one direction having to be compensated by a countervailing move along another dimension.[2]

The EU is a standard illustration where countries have opted for a substantial degree of fixity of their exchange rates[3] (*vis-a-vis* each other) with free capital mobility in place but monetary policy independence sacrificed. This is partly attributable to the EU constituting an optimum currency area in Mundell's (1961) sense and also to their being subject to similar "shocks" (see *Bayoumi and Eichengreen* (1992)). But this must be regarded as an exceptional case. Typically countries would be reluctant to sacrifice monetary policy autonomy, for reasons of national sovereignty and national pride, and the effective choice thus narrows down to that between capital mobility and a fixed exchange rate regime.

For the advanced economies the choice seems to be clear (at least to most academics and policy-makers) viz. the benefits of capital mobility and independent monetary policy exceed whatever costs may be associated with a system of freely floating exchange rates. For the LDCs and EMEs, the picture becomes more hazy. One view (see *Vegh* (1992), *Dornbusch and Warner* (1994), Bernanke (2005)) maintains that the best course for such economies is to overcome their deeply ingrained *"fear of floating"* and let the exchange rate float freely. A firm central bank commitment to gear monetary policy exclusively to maintaining a low and stable inflation rate, would then provide the much needed *"nominal anchor"* for the macroeconomic system. There are two major arguments against a *"free float"* for such economies.

(i) Firstly, as Sargent (1982) has noted, a fixed (or heavily managed) exchanged rate can be a suitable guard against high inflation, and can even act as a strong brake on persistent hyperinflations.[4] A fixed exchange rate commands visibility and is more credible than a direct inflation target (both because the former is observable instantaneously unlike the inflation rate which suffers from a lag of at least a few weeks and also because its measurement is non-controversial in contrast to the several competing measures suggested for the inflation rate in the literature).

(ii) Secondly, Calvo and Reinhart (2000) have drawn attention to the low credibility of policy-makers in several LDCs, which could mean that a flexible exchange rate could exhibit high volatility (both short-term and long-term). The latter is usually recognized as exports inhibiting and could also lead to volatility of capital inflows and in domestic interest rates (if these are unregulated) via the covered interest parity (*Calvo* (1996), *Kwack* (2003), *Cavoli and Rajan* (2006), etc.).

In the Indian context, the problems confronting monetary policy in the wake of capital inflows (and financial liberalization generally) have been discussed extensively in Rangarajan (2000), Reddy (2005), Mohan (2007), Nachane and Raje (2007), etc. There has been in evidence a general movement away from a heavily managed exchange rate system of the 1980s and early 1990s towards. Today the concerns over the exchange rate are limited to short-term considerations such as the need to smoothen out excessive volatility and foreclose the emergence of destabilizing speculative activities and are usually subsumed under the rubric of *"overall financial stability"*. However even though the RBI does not have a target exchange rate band in mind, it has not hesitated from pro-active intervention to prevent undue nominal exchange rate intervention. However such episodes of *"leaning against the wind"* are becoming increasingly less frequent now as the economy is showing signs of a robust growth and successful integration with the international economy. However as the following quotation from Mohan (2007) illustrates, India's exchange rate policy is in a state of evolution and may undergo a substantial transformation in the foreseeable future.

> *".. the Dutch disease syndrome has so far been managed by way of reserves build-up and sterilization, the former preventing excessive nominal appreciation and the latter preventing higher inflation. However the issue remains how long and to what extent such an exchange rate management strategy would work given the fact that we are faced with large and continuing capital flows apart from strengthening current receipts on account of remittances and software exports."*[5]

3. CAC: MACROECONOMIC EFFECTS ON THE REAL ECONOMY

3.1 IMF's Financial Programming Model

The transmission mechanism through which short-term capital flows impinge on the real economy are at best imperfectly understood. The major features of the IMF's Financial Programming Model may be described in the following terms. We have firstly the national accounting identity

$$(I_G - S_G) + (I_P - S_P) = \Delta D - \Delta A - \Delta R \quad (1)$$

This simply states that the excess of government investment (I_G) over government saving (S_G) together with the corresponding excess of private investment (I_P) over private saving (S_P) must be balanced by the excess of changes in the long-term external debt and foreign investment stocks (ΔD) over the combined changes in the short-term asset positions of non-residents and in forex reserves ($\Delta A + \Delta R$)

Additionally, we have the definitional identities

$$S_P = (Y - T) - C \quad (2)$$

$$S_G = (T - G) \quad (3)$$

where T represents government taxes, G is government current expenditure, and Y is national income.

Combining the above three equations lead to the following:

$$(I_G + G - T) + (I_P + C - Y + T) = (M - X) = \Delta D - \Delta A - \Delta R \quad (4)$$

where M, X are the imports and exports respectively.

Models building on various extensions of the above basic framework [see *Rao and Nallari* (2001) for a detailed overview] have been used to justify the IMF case for freer capital movements. Let us examine a few of these propositions critically.

A persuasive critique of the IMF model derives from the asymmetric information, moral hazard and agency literature (see *Stiglitz and Weiss* (1992), *Grandmont* (1998), etc.). This critique comprises three key components:

1. Domestic capital markets in several LDCs and EMEs lack "efficiency", plagued as they are by *agency* and *asymmetric information* problems.
2. Secondly, financial liberalization involves in its wake a large-scale conversion of liquid into illiquid assets, and the associated risks are not reflected in interest rates due to the adverse selection phenomenon. In the face of incomplete financial markets, large imbalances tend to be thrown onto the most liquid market (viz. that for foreign securities).
3. Interest rates in small open economies (under CAC) are not determined by the marginal productivity of capital or the intersection of the savings and investment schedules. Instead they are more likely to be determined by an interest parity condition of the form

$$i_d = i_w + \left(\frac{f^e - f}{f}\right) + \theta \qquad (5)$$

where i_d, i_w are respectively domestic and world interest rates, f^e, f are the expected and actual values of the exchange rate and θ a country risk factor.

By virtue of (5), it is clear that the domestic rate of interest does not act as a market-clearing mechanism, but depends on several of the same factors that determine short-term capital flows, lending a dimension of instability to the exchange rate and the balance of payments generally.

3.2 Virtuous (International) Debt Cycle

The cornerstone of the IMF's prescription of CAC relates to the assuaging of the fears of several potential LDC liberalizers on the debt trap syndrome. The FP (Financial

Programming) model referred to above often serves as the basis for a demonstration of the so-called "virtuous debt cycle" whereby capital inflows raise domestic investment (by bridging the *savings and forex gaps*), and thereby domestic output. Subsequently, a domestic surplus (through increased tax yields or private profits) emerges which translates either into a current account surplus (or at least a reduced deficit), thus liquidating the initial foreign loan. However as Devlin *et al.* (1995) have shown, for the mechanism described above to be sustainable the following four conditions need to be fulfilled:

(i) $\left(\frac{dI}{dA}\right) \succ \left(\frac{dC}{dA}\right)$

where I is the total investment in the economy (i.e. ($I = I_G + I_P$).

This condition requires that short-term capital inflows should augment investment more than consumption.

(ii) $\left(\frac{dY}{dA}\right) \succ 1$

The resulting investment should augment factor productivity.

(iii) $\left(\frac{dX}{dA}\right) \succ \left(\frac{dM}{dA}\right)$

The new investment must lead to a net export surplus.

(iv) $\left(\frac{dS}{dY}\right) \succ \left(\frac{S}{Y}\right)$

The marginal savings rate must exceed the average savings rate.

We do not go into a detailed discussion of these conditions but *prima facie* they appear to be fairly restrictive and somewhat difficult of fulfilment in the context of most LDCs (see e.g. *Reisen* (1996)). Our only purpose is to stress that the prescriptions following from the FP model do not apply unconditionally.

3.3 Fluctuations in Public Investment

Capital flows can have pronounced impacts on the fiscal budget, principally on its capital investment component. These effects are transmitted through two major channels—

1. Exchange rate variations can have important effects on the budget mainly through the costs of external debt servicing. To the extent that capital inflows lead to an exchange rate appreciation, there is a reduction in this servicing costs, so that the influence of capital inflows on this count must be regarded as benign.
2. Another important channel of transmission is via the influence of domestic interest rates. In theory capital inflows should cause domestic interest rates to fall, but usually this tendency is kept in check by the monetary authority through sterilization operations. As capital inflows accelerate, the perceived country risk factor θ in (5) could move sharply upwards raising domestic interest rates. Besides capital inflows are usually accompanied by financial liberalization on a broad-front, and this is very often associated with an upward interest rate movement. The rise in domestic interest rates impinges heavily on the internal debt servicing requirements of the government.

The net impact of the above two factors is difficult to determine but there are strong *a priori* reasons for supposing that the second effect might be the dominant one. Fitzgerald and Mavrotas (1997) develop an analytical model in which the crucial variable is the *solvency ratio* λ which foreign investors regard as desirable for a country. This ratio λ is volatile and dependent on the state of investor expectations. The investors' desire to see the actual solvency ratio below their desired level, translates into demands for a strong fiscal surplus, and domestic governments faced with inflexible revenues and limited elbow room for manoeuvring current expenditure, inevitably take recourse to trimming capital expenditure. Two factors typically exacerbate this tendency. Firstly, the classical tenet of public finance that the revenue budget should be in balance (a tenet which is a prominent component of our FRBM Act) and secondly, the fact that capital expenditures (except on the defence account) are so much easier to prune politically.

3.4 Effects on Output and Growth

The relationship between capital account liberalization and economic growth has been debated at great length both theoretically and empirically. Summers (2000), Fischer (1998), Kaminsky and Schmukler (2002) make out the standard new-classical case for financial liberalization in general and capital account liberalization in particular. But this view ignores several key features of the ground reality in a majority of LDCs and EMEs. In these countries, security markets are not the major source of long-term industrial finance. Instead, firms are bank-dependent for their working capital funds, whereas their long-term funding comes from either internal funds (i.e. retained funds) or external borrowing (including foreign borrowing). Because equity markets are narrow and shallow, they exhibit wide fluctuations in response to changes in foreign flows. Such fluctuations in turn affect the availability of bank credit (unless fully sterilized), real exchange rate movements, and interest rates (via monetary policy responses). As shown in Fitzgerald and Mavratos (1997) such oscillations tend to magnify the effects of financial frictions originating abroad on the domestic economy, without having any compensatory positive effect on private sector fixed capital formation. Aghion *et al.* (2000) qualify such conclusions by noting that capital account liberalization is deleterious only when it is premature (i.e. when undertaken without adequate financial development).

Given the conflicting theoretical picture, it is of interest to turn to the empirical evidence. Here one immediately runs into the problem of developing a suitable measure of capital account liberalization. At least four measures have been suggested in the literature which we briefly list below.

(i) *IMF measure (CAL1)*: The IMF publishes annually the *Report on Exchange Arrangements and Exchange Restrictions*, wherein line E.2 lists the status country-wise on each of 13 major capital account transactions. The measure CAL1 is simply the *proportion of years in the sample period in which controls were absent*, and is thus a number between 0 and 1.

(ii) *Quinn's Measure (CAL2)*: Quinn's (1997) measure is also based on the IMF data but attempts to give weightage to the intensity of the controls. Thus a score of 0 indicates both receipts and payments forbidden (on any of the transactions), 0.5 indicates some regulatory restrictions, 1 indicates heavy taxes, 1.5 moderate taxes and 2 no taxes. The measure is calculated for each year (it is between 0 and 4—the sum of the values of the two separate categories of receipts and payments). We call this measure as CAL2, and this has the advantage (unlike CAL1) that it is defined for every year rather than only over a sample period. As such it can be used conveniently as a time series to indicate the progression of capital account liberalization in any given country.

(iii) *Montiel-Reinhart (1999) Measure (CAL3)*: This indicator is similar to Quinn's measure, but varies only between 0 and 2. A value of 0 indicates a "no restrictions" situation, 1 represents "overzealous potential restrictions" (e.g. limits on forex exposure of banks) while 2 indicates the existence of "explicit measures" (financial transactions taxes, deposit requirements, prohibitions, etc.).

(iv) *Uncovered Interest Parity Measures (CAL4)*: Reisen and Yeches (1993) suggested a measure of capital account openness based on the UIP (uncovered interest parity). Let i* denote the UIP interest rate, i_d the actual domestic interest rate, and i′ the hypothetical closed economy interest rate. CAL4 is then defined as in the following equation:

$$i_d = \mu i^* + (1-\mu) i' \quad (6)$$

Table 1 presents the main features of some empirical studies designed to explain the growth implications of capital account liberalization. Most of the studies employ panel data on sets of countries in the post-Bretton Woods era. While Table 1 lays no claim to exhaustiveness, it does indicate that the case for capital account openness being growth enhancing is far from convincing and that whatever benefits may be involved are confined to high-income countries, though even the latter conclusion is challenged by empirical investigations such as those of Eatwell (1996) and Singh (1997).

3.5 Other Important Distortions

Capital account liberalization introduces several other potential sources of distortion, of which we note the following:

(i) One of the most important distortions is the steep rise in asset prices as foreign capital pours into important asset markets such as equities and real estate. The problem becomes particularly sensitive with the real estate market. In countries experiencing demographic as well as urbanization pressures, there is a chronic shortage of urban housing. Hence it is a safe bet that real estate prices have a strong upward trend. Foreign capital on the look out for capital gains finds housing investment an attractive option. The investment is both on the demand and supply side. That foreign purchases of property push up prices would be obvious. Equally obvious is the fact that the poor and middle-class domestic buyers (whose salaries would be indexed, if at all, to a price index which does not incorporate housing prices) would find themselves rapidly priced out of the housing market. What is not so obvious is the fact that even foreign investment in real estate development does not really relieve this distress but actually aggravates it as this estate development essentially involves constructing condominiums that cater to tastes (and budgets) of the upper segments of the society (and of course non-residents). As a matter of fact, such estate development very often blocks off any increase in the supply of effective housing space for the poor and the middle-class. This phenomenon is rampant in most LDCs and EMEs and India constitutes a prime example.

(ii) A real exchange rate appreciation could result from an upward pressure on the asset prices. This could act as an important retardant of exports and undermine the progress of trade reforms.

(iii) As discussed in Fernandez-Arias and Montiel (1996), distortions to the perceived cost of foreign capital may arise because of externalities associated with aggregate country risk and credit rationing arising from limited *cross-border contract enforceability*.

(iv) Distortions in the financial sector could give rise to improper financial intermediation (*Calvo et al.* (1993)) and result in excessive foreign borrowing.

Several further instances of macroeconomic and microeconomic distortions that can result from capital flows are discussed in Corbo and Hernadez (1996).

4. CAPITAL ACCOUNT LIBERALIZATION IN INDIA: A STATUS REPORT

4.1 First CAC Committee (Tarapore I)

To put our discussion in perspective, let us commence by reviewing a few empirical facts about capital flows and forex markets. The global forex market has an average daily turnover of US $ 1.88 trillion (as of 2004) according to the latest Triennial Central Bank Survey of Foreign Exchange and Derivatives Market Activity by the BIS (2005). This makes the forex market the largest financial market in the world.[6] The main participants in this forex market are central, commercial and investment banks, hedge funds, pension funds, corporations and individuals, with more than 75% of the transactions being routed through banks. The U.K., U.S. and Japan account for the largest shares in the daily turnover (see Table 2). Table 3 shows that the major trade occurs in four currencies viz. the US dollar, Euro, Sterling, and the Japanese Yen, accounting between themselves for 78% of the total cross-currency trade with the Euro-US$ share the highest (at 28%). The spot market accounts for about one-third of the daily turnover (US $621 billion), with *foreign exchange swaps* being the largest component (at US $944 billion), followed by *outright forwards* (at US $ 208 billion).

Capital inflows into India have been increasing ever since the reforms were initiated, but there has been a marked acceleration in theses inflows—both of the FDI (foreign direct investment) and FPI (foreign portfolio investment) variety. As indicated in Table 4, total foreign investment during the year 2005-06 stood at approximately US $20 billion with FPI accounting for nearly 62% of this total. The rate of growth of FDI is considerably lower than that of FPI, though (as expected) the latter shows greater volatility. Shortly before the onset of the Asian crisis in June 1997, a committee to lay down a roadmap for moving to full capital account convertibility was appointed under the Chairmanship of S.S. Tarapore. We will refer to this Committee as Tarapore I. The Committee adopted a three-fold approach.

Firstly, it enumerated the major kinds of restrictions that were in force in India for capital account transactions.

For this purpose, it grouped these restrictions according to the sector that they were applied to viz. (i) Corporates (Domestic/Resident), (ii) Corporates (Foreign/Non-Resident), (iii) Banks (Domestic/Resident), (iv) Banks (Foreign/Non-Resident), (v) Non Bank Financial Institutions (Resident), (vi) Non-Bank Financial Institutions (Non-Resident) or what are now popularly called as FIIs (foreign institutional investors), (vii) Individual (Residents), (viii) Individulas (Non-Residents), and (ix) Financial Markets

Secondly the Committee laid down a framework for the progressive dismantling of each of these restrictions over a short span of three years (i.e. by April 2000).

Thirdly, it laid down a series of macroeconomic conditions that needed to be fulfilled before CAC was finally attained. These conditions are listed in Table 5 (together with the position obtaining on each of them as at end of 2005-06, i.e. 6 years after CAC was supposed to be in place).

4.2 Second CAC Committee (Tarapore II)

The Asian crisis cast the entire issue of capital account liberalization in a fresh perspective. As Goldstein (1998), Singh (2002), Bhalla and Nachane (2001), etc. have noted the extent of capital account liberalization made a big difference to the incidence of the crisis on individual countries, and countries like India and China managed to avoid the worst consequences of the crisis mainly because their capital accounts still had a number of restrictions in place. The sobering effects of the crisis meant that the recommendations of Tarapore I had to be shelved for a few years subsequent to the crisis.

However, following the high growth phase of the last few years, Indian policy-makers once again began flirting with the CAC idea. A new committee was hastily set up once again under the Chairmanship of S.S. Tarapore, with many notable "champions" of CAC on board.[7] We will refer to this Committee as Tarapore II. This Committee once again followed an approach much similar in spirit to that of the earlier Committee. It began by reviewing the extent to which the earlier Committee's recommendations had been actually implemented. It then laid down a detailed time-frame for achieving full convertibility and also drew out a new set of safety guidelines. Let us turn briefly to each of these aspects in turn.

Table 6 is an *"action taken report"* on the major recommendations of Tarapore I. It shows that most of the recommendations have been either followed or even exceeded. So one may say that there has already been a *"creeping movement"* in the direction of CAC. However, Tarapore II is far more ambitious in the scope of its recommendations, and intends to take India quite a bit further along the road to full (or almost full) capital account convertibility. This it proposes to do progressively in three phases: Phase I (2006-07), Phase II (2007-09) and Phase III (2009-11). The major recommendations of Tarapore II are set out below:

1. Removal of overall ECB ceiling of US $ 22 billion and removal of restrictions on end-use of ECBs.
2. Limits on corporate investments abroad be doubled from the current limit of 200% of net worth.
3. Banks be allowed to borrow overseas upto 50% of paid-up capital and reseves in Phase I, which amount can be raised to 75% in Phase II and 100% in Phase III.
4. As against the current limit of $25,000, individuals be allowed to remit abroad (annually) upto $50,000 in Phase I, $ 100,000 in Phase II and $200,000 in Phase III.
5. Currently only NRIs are allowed to invest in companies listed on Indian stock exchanges. The Committee recommends extension of this facility to all non-residents (through SEBI registered entities such as mutual funds and other portfolio management schemes).
6. FIIs be *prohibited* from raising money through Participatory Notes (PNs).

4.3 The Issue of Participatory Notes

As noted above, Tarapore II has explicitly demanded a

ban on PNs. However, this was not a unanimous decision of the Committee. As a matter of fact, two members had submitted notes of dissent. The issue is a rather controversial one, especially as the RBI and the Finance Ministry view it from radically different perspectives. PNs are instruments similar to contract notes issued by registered FIIs to overseas clients, who are not directly eligible to invest in Indian securities markets. The PNs are issued against an underlying security thereby helping the holder to benefit from dividends and capital gains on that security. The RBI stand on PNs was first articulated when the RBI member entered a note of dissent to the Lahiri Committee Report on *Liberalization of Foreign Institutional Investment* (2004). The RBI's case for banning PNs is based on the fact that the nature of the beneficiary or the identity of the investor is unknown, unlike in the case of FIIs registered with a financial regulator. Most of the PNs are issued to hedge funds, with opaque ownership and shifting location, which are not registered in any country or with any regulator.[8] The Lahiri Committee on the contrary, felt that the current regulations for PNs are adequate, as (with effect from 3 Feb. 2004) PNs can be issued only to regulated entities, and the FIIs issuing PNs are bound by KYC (know your customer) norms. In my opinion there are two major considerations which weigh the argument in favour of the RBI's point of view. Firstly, the enforcement of KYC norms is difficult because several hedge funds operate in unregulated countries behind a veil of confidentiality provisions. Even reputed institutions operate through subsidiaries in Mauritius and often stonewall on provision of information. Secondly, and even more importantly, as pointed out by M.K. Narayanan (National Security Advisor, Government of India) in a speech at the *43rd Munich Conference on Security Policy* (2007) terrorist organizations have been increasingly resorting to legitimate business enterprises and routine banking channels to fund their outfits. PNs could be thus providing a safe conduit for the movement of terrorist funding.

4.4 Safety Guidelines

One welcome feature of Tarapore II is the recognition

that the bold recommendations it has made, would need an extensive safety network in place. It thus goes to great lengths towards suggesting several measures in the money market, corporate bond market, government securities market and forex market. What is worrisome, however, is that most of these measures, while supposedly masquerading as "safety guidelines" seem specifically designed to weaken regulatory mechanisms in important segments of these markets. They thus seem more in the nature of "accompaniments" to CAC rather than "prudential" measures. The Committee has virtually nothing to say on instruments designed to insulate financial markets and the macroeconomy from the destabilizing consequences of capital inflows.

5. MEASURES FOR COPING WITH CAPITAL INFLOWS

Irrespective of whether India decides to go for full CAC or otherwise, management of capital inflows will remain an important issue. One rational policy response would then be to examine a minimal set of capital account restrictions that will mitigate the probability of financial crises of the order of the Asian Crisis (1997-98), the LTCM crisis (1998) or the Russian crisis (1998). We examine a few such proposals below.

5.1 Tobin Taxes

Perhaps the oldest such proposal is the Tobin tax, suggested by Tobin (1978) in an influential article, though the idea itself can be traced back even further viz. to the following specific passage occurring in Keynes's General Theory (1936) (p. 160):

> *"The introduction of a substantial Government transfer tax on all transactions might prove the most serviceable reform available, with a view to mitigating the dominance of speculation over enterprise in the United States"*

The transactions tax rate usually proposed (*Tobin* (1978), *Summers and Summers* (1990), *Spahn* (1996), etc.) typically range from 0.05% to 0.25% of the transaction principal. The burden of the tax is inversely related to the length of the holding period.[9] Although the rate is small, as shown by Dodd (2002) it amounts to a substantial proportional increase in current transactions costs, as the typical bid-ask spreads in inter-dealer markets are between 0.01% to 0.04% (of the principal). The tax can thus be expected to reduce the returns to short-term speculation. This would be a double-edged weapon, as it would simultaneously reduce the volume of speculative *hot money* and reduce forex volatility. Additionally, it could generate substantial revenue which could be available for development purposes.[10]

In spite of its intellectual appeal, however, as a practical proposal it has not really got-off the ground. There could be several reasons for this. Firstly, the proposal would require worldwide agreement and coordination. Otherwise funds will simply migrate to countries which opt out of the tax agreement[11] There is also a distribution problem, for most of the revenue will accrue to the developed Western economies. Finally, unless the tax is applied to both the spot capital flows as well as the derivative instruments (forwards, futures, options and swaps), there may be substitution from the former to the latter.

5.2 Trip Wires-Speed Bumps Approach (TW-SB)

The essence of this approach is simple. Certain basic indicators (TWs) are defined and as and when these indicators deteriorate (below a threshold) certain safety measures (relating to capital account transactions) are "triggered-off". The approach has been exciting increasing interest among economists in recent years (see *Ariyoshi et al.* (2000), *Grabel* (2003), etc.). The TWs are usually simple indicators that are designed to warn policy-makers of impending risks. Among suggested TWs[12] we may prominently mention:

(i) Ratio of official reserves to total short-term external obligations (foreign portfolio investment and total—i.e. private plus public—short-term hard-currency denominated foreign debt).

(ii) Ratio of foreign currency denominated debt to domestic currency denominated debt (appropriately weighted by maturity).
(iii) Ratio of short-term debt to long-term debt.
(iv) Ratio of total cumulative foreign portfolio investment to gross equity market capitalization.

Under the approach, whenever TWs cross predetermined critical thresholds, various SBs are called into play. The latter could take several forms including—

(i) requirements on borrowers to unwind positions involving locational/maturity mismatches,
(ii) curbs on foreign borrowings,
(iii) restrictions on certain types of FPI, and
(iv) import curbs (in exceptional circumstances).

5.3 The Chilean Model

Chile is widely touted as a successful example of a financial liberalization programme, but it has to be remembered that a large role in the Chilean success story is attributable to an extremely cautious approach to capital inflows that was followed from May 1992 to October 1998, and which represented an ingenious combination of the Tobin and TW-SB approaches.

Central to the Chilean approach was an extremely flexible model of capital flows regulation, which incorporated five main features:

(i) A tax of 1.2% per annum on external commercial loans,
(ii) A one-year residence requirement for FDI,
(iii) A non-interest bearing reserve requirement of 30% on all types of external credits and all foreign financial investment in the country,
(iv) An exchange rate band with occasional movements permitted in the central parity rate (similar to the *snake in the tunnel arrangement* prevailing in Western Europe prior to the formation of the EMU), and

(v) A restriction on outflows of Pension Funds to a maximum of 12% of their assets abroad.

The Chilean model may be regarded as a highly effective means for managing the various types of risks associated with capital account liberalization (see Section 2.3 above).

Currency risk was managed via a crawling peg arrangement complemented by inflows management. As a result the Chilean currency appreciation and current account deficit were smaller than in other Latin American countries. Hence the currency never came under attack following the Asian and Mexican crises.

Flight risk was mitigated by discouraging those inflows that carried the maximum risk, with the reserve requirements acting as a type of Tobin tax on these investments.

The minimum resident requirement on FDI reinforced long-term investments, while barricading the entry of short-term flows disguised as FDI. This effective bias against short-term capital inflows went quite some way towards containing *fragility* and *contagion risks*.

In sum, these controls played a major role in insulating the Chilean economy from the global financial turbulence of the 1990s. The most notable feature of this win-win situation is that Chile received a larger proportion of external finance (relative to GDP) as compared to other countries in the region, with FDI constituting a larger portion of the inflows than in many EMEs.

These controls had to be abandoned in 1998 in the wake of the pronounced decline in foreign inflows brought about by the combination of the Asian, Russian and LTCM crises, but there is no doubt that the Chilean model deserves careful consideration from other EMEs too.

6. CONCLUSION

In recent years EMEs are facing increasing pressures from multilateral institutions and developed countries to liberalize their capital accounts. This case essentially rests on five claims made on behalf of capital account liberalization.

(i) Such liberalization achieves the optimum allocation of global financial resources, letting capital flow to those regions where its marginal productivity is highest. It thus helps EMEs to raise the rate of capital formation above their domestic savings rate.

(ii) Capital inflows promote long-term growth in EMEs by contributing to transfer of technology, financial know-how and management skills.

(iii) Capital inflows have a disciplining effect on domestic fiscal and monetary policy.

(iv) Capital inflows dampen the effects of exogenous shocks on the domestic economy.

(v) Free mobility of financial capital is essential for stimulating global trade.

Several of these claims are sustained in terms of the IMF's Financial Programming model. However, as we have noted in this paper, the IMF model is subject to important caveats stemming from moral hazard, asymmetric information and agency problems. Admitting these caveats casts serious doubts on several of the above claims. Besides, there are the special problems created by short-term capital mobility in terms of financial market instability, asset bubbles and other micro-economic distortions. These problems are not a new discovery, and as a matter of fact were noted by Keynes in his *General Theory* seventy years ago, as stemming from the special nature of asset markets such as *"animal spirits"* and *"herd behaviour"*. The efficient markets theory, advanced as an alternative to Keynes' somber view of financial markets, fails to address the issue of the destabilizing effects on financial markets of speculative behaviour by "noisy traders". There is thus sufficient ground to cast doubts on the theoretical case for capital account liberalization.

The empirical evidence is not very reassuring either. Capital account liberalization has occasionally proved beneficial, but only for relatively developed countries, and only if accompanied by appropriate prudential measures in the financial system. In the Indian context the government has shown a keenness for accelerating capital account liberalization and going all out for full CAC. The two committees appointed to examine the issue (Tarapore I and II) have laid out a detailed roadmap for CAC, along with the necessary safeguards. To this author, it is not very evident that these committees (especially Tarapore II) have really gone into a detailed examination of all the risks attached to CAC, and devoted sufficient attention to measures such as TWSBs which have recently been experimented with in several countries. It is important to stress that the line taken by several apologists for CAC that the risks of financial instability is negligible and hence more than compensated for by the benefits ignores the magnitude of the potential costs of a crisis.[13]

The TWSB measures have three special features:

(i) They can prove highly effective in insulating economies from financial crises, without impinging seriously on the volume of FDI (though it will act as a curb on short-term capital flows).

(ii) They would be more effective in checking real currency appreciation and prove cheaper than the conventional sterilization measures usually invoked to deal with capital inflows.

(iii) Contrary to fears expressed in certain quarters, such controls need not necessarily increase the cost of foreign capital to EMEs. As a matter of fact, with effective controls in place (and the corresponding reduced vulnerability to crises), the risk premium on foreign capital is likely to decrease.

The overwhelming evidence against CAC, however, may not necessarily convince some of the *die-hard reformers* among India's current economic policy-makers. Since this group has conveniently decided to regard all advice emanating from resident Indian economists as otiose, I can do no better in conclusion, than to quote from one of the leading architects of the erstwhile Washington Consensus:

"At this stage full capital account liberalization promises no large benefits, while it increases the risk of things going badly wrong"—John Williamson (2006).

Notes and References

1. The most common assumptions underpinning new classical economics are: (i) rational expectations, (ii) market clearing, and (iii) macro-economy assumed to possess a unique full employment equilibrium.
2. Obstfeld *et al.* (2004), present several historical instances of the trilemma.
3. The euro is, however, floating against the other major currencies such as the US dollar and the Japanese yen.
4. He cites the role of exchange rate stabilization in ending the 1920s European hyperinflation.
5. The introduction of the MSS (Market Stabilization Scheme) in April 2004 assumes significance in this context as an important tool for short-term liquidity management.
6. This forex turnover is more than 10 times the daily turnover of global equity markets (at $167 billion), 40 times the daily turnover of the NYSE (at $46 billion) and on an annual basis the forex turnover is more than 10 times the value of the combined world GDP (estimated at $36 trillion).
7. As a matter of fact, notwithstanding the fact that the Committee Chairman was a highly respected senior central banker, well known for his independent views, the general feeling was that the composition of the Committee was loaded heavily in favour of the officially desired result—a stratagem increasingly resorted to by Indian governments in the past two decades.
8. PNs currently constitute about 25% of net portfolio investment.
9. For example, a tax of 0.10% implies that a twice daily round trip carries an annual rate of interest of 146%, whereas the same figure for a twice weekly round trip reduces sharply to about 21%.
10. D'Orville and Najman (1995) estimate that a Tobin tax of 0.25% would globally fetch a revenue of US $140 billion, whereas Felix and Sau (1996) predict the revenue generation at over twice this amount (for the same rate).
11. The phenomenal rise of the Eurodollar market in the 1980s should serve to remind us of the scale of transactions that can occur outside a system of central bank clearing.
12. There are also special types of TWs called "contagion TWs" which are activated in a given country (say A) whenever SBs are invoked in another country (say B). Such TWs become especially important for groups of countries with interdependent financial systems in general and interlocked funds in particular.

13. As given in Mohan (2007), recapitalization of banks (subsequent to the financial crises of the 1990s) cost 55% of GDP in Argentina, 42% in Thailand, 35% in Korea and 10% in Turkey. The total welfare costs would be substantially higher.

References

Aghion, P., P. Bacchetta and A. Banerjee (2000): "Currency Crises and Monetary Policy in an Economy with Credit Constraints," *CEPR Discussion Paper No. 2529.*

Ariyoshi, A. *et al.* (2000): "Capital Controls: Country Experiences with their Use and Liberalization", *IMF Occasional Paper No. 190.*

Bayoumi, T. and B.Eichengreen (1993), "Shocking aspects of European Monetary Integration" in G. Torres and F. Giavazzi (ed.), *Adjustment and Growth in European Monetary Union*, Cambridge University Press, Cambridge, UK.

Bernanke, B.S. (2005): "Monetary Policy in a World of Mobile Capital", *Cato Journal*, Vol. 25(1), pp. 1-12.

Bhalla, A.S. and D.M. Nachane (2001): "The Economic Import of the Asian Crisis in India and China", in H. Chang, G. Palma and D.H. Whittaker (ed.), *Financial Liberalization and the Asian Crisis*, Palgrave, New York, 2001.

Boughton, J. (1997): "From Suez to Tequila: The IMF as Crisis Manager", *IMF, Working Paper No. WP/97/90.*

Calvo, G. (1996): "Capital Flows and Macroeconomic Management: Tequila Lessons", *International Journal of Finance and Economics*, Vol. 1(3), pp. 207-23.

Calvo, G., L. Leiderman and C. Reinhart (1993): "Capital inflows and real exchange rate appreciation in Latin America", *IMF Staff Papers*, Vol. 40 (March), pp. 108-51.

Calvo, G. and C. Reinhart (2000): "Fear of Floating", *NBER Working Paper No. 7993.*

Cavoli, T. and R.S. Rajan (2006): "Capital inflows problem in selected Asian economies in the 1990s revisited: The role of monetary sterilization", *Asian Economic Journal*, Vol. 20(4), pp. 409-23.

Chesnais, F. (1994): *La Mondialisation du Capital*, Syros, Paris.

Corbo, V. and L.Hernandez (1996): "Macroeconomic adjustment to capital inflows: Lessons from recent Latin American and East Asian experience", *The World Bank Research Observer*, Vol. 11(1), pp. 61-85.

Demirguc-Kunt, A. and E. Detragiache (1998): "Financial Liberalization and Financial Fragility," *IMF Working Paper No. 98/83.*

Devlin, R. (1989): *Debt Crisis in Latin America: The Supply Side of the Story*, Princeton University Press, Princeton.

Devlin, R., R. Ffrench-Davis and S. Griffith-Jones (1995): "Surges in capital flows and development" in R. Ffrench-Davis and S. Griffith-Jones (ed.), *Coping with Capital Surges: The Return of Finance to Latin America*, Lynne Reimer Publishers, Boulder, CO.

Diaz-Alexandro, C. (1985): "Goodbye financial repression, hello financial crash", *Journal of Development Economics*, Vol. 19(1), pp. 1-24

Dodd, R. (2002): *Lessons for Tobin Tax Advocates: The Politics of Policy and the Economics of Market Micro-Structure, Financial Policy Forum*, Special Report No. 7, Washington, D.C.

Dornbusch, R. and A. Warner (1994): " Mexico: Stabilization, reform and no growth", *Brookings Papers on Economic Activity*, No. 1, pp. 253-315.

D'Orville, H. and D. Najman (1995): *Towards a New Multilateralism: Funding Global Priorities*, United Nations, New York.

Eatwell, J. (1996): "International Capital Liberalization: The Impact on World Development," Schwarz Centre for Economic Policy Analysis (SCEPA), New School University, *Working Paper No. 1996-02.*

Eichengreen, B. (1996): "Institutions and economic growth: Europe after World War II" in N. Crafts and G. Toniolo (ed.), *Economic Growth in Europe since 1945*, Cambridge University Press, Cambridge.

Felix, D. (1995): "Financial Globalization versus Free Trade: The Case for the Tobin Tax," *UNCTAD Discussion Paper No. 108.*

Felix, D. (1998): "On drawing general policy lessons from recent Latin American currency crises", *Journal of Post-Keynesian Economics*, Vol. 20(2), pp. 191-221.

Felix, D. and R. Sau (1996): "On the revenue potential and phasing in of the Tobin tax " in M. Haq, I. Kaul and I. Grunberg (ed.), *The Tobin Tax: Coping with Financial Viability*, Oxford University Press, New York.

Filardo, A.J. (2000): "Monetary policy and asset prices", *FRB of Kansas City Economic Review*, Vol. 85(3), pp. 11-37.

Fisher, S. (1998): *Should the International Monetary Fund Pursue Capital Account Convertibility?, Essays in International Finance*, 207, Princeton University.

FitzGerald, E. and G. Mavrotas (1997), *International Capital Flows, Investment and Employment in Developing Countries*, ILO, Geneva.

Goldstein, M. (1998): "The Asian Financial Crisis: Causes, Cures and Systemic Implication", *Policy Analyses in International Economics*, Vol. 55, Peterson Institute for International Economics.

Goodfriend, M. (2005): "The monetary policy debate since October 1979: Lessons for theory and practice", *FRB of St. Louis Review*, Vol. 87 (2), pp. 243-62.

Government of India (Ministry of Finance) (2004): *Report of the Committee on Liberalization of Foreign Institutional Investment*, (Lahiri Committee).

Grabel, I. (2003): "Averting crisis: Assessing means to manage financial integration in emerging economies", *Cambridge Journal of Economics*, Vol. 27(2), pp. 317-36.

Grandmont, J.M. (1998): "Introduction to market psychology and non-linear endogenous business cycles", *Journal of Economic Theory*, Vol. 80(1), pp. 1-13.

Huberman, G. and T. Regev (2001): "Contagious speculation and a cure for cancer: A non-event that made prices soar", *Journal of Finance*, Vol. 56(1), pp. 387-96.

Kahneman, D. and A. Tversky (1984): "Choices, values and frames", *American Psychologist*, Vol. 39(4), pp. 341-50.

Kaminsky, G.L. and C.L. Reinhart (1999): "The twin crises: The causes of banking and balance-of-payments problems", *American Economic Review*, Vol. 89(3), pp. 473-500.

Kaminsky, G.L. and S.L. Schmukler (1998): "Short-run pain, long-run gain: The effects of financial liberalization", Paper presented at The World Bank Conference on *Financial globalization: A Blessing or a Curse?*

Keynes, J.M. (1936): *The General Theory of Employment, Interest and Money*, Harcourt Jovanovich, London.

Khan, M.S. and N.U. Haque (1990): "Adjustment with growth: Relating the analytical approaches of the IMF and the World Bank", *Journal of Development Economics*, Vol. 32(1), pp. 155-79.

Kwack, S. (2003): "An empirical assessment of monetary policy responses to capital inflows in East Asia before the Crisis", *International Economic Journal*, Vol. 15(1), pp. 95-113.

LeRoy, S.F. and R.D. Porter (1981): "The present value relation: Tests based on implied variance bounds", *Econometrica*, Vol. 49(3), pp. 555-74.

Mohan, R. (2007): "Capital account liberalization and conduct of monetary policy: The Indian experience", Paper presented at a Seminar on *Globalization, Inflation and Financial Markets* (Banque de France, Paris, France, 14 June 2007)

Montiel, P. and C. Reinhart (1999): "Do capital controls and macroeconomic policies influence the volume and composition of capital flows ? Evidence from the 1990s", *Journal of International Money and Finance*, Vol. 18(4), pp. 619-35.

Mundell, R. (1961): "A theory of optimum currency areas", *American Economic Review*, Vol. 51 (4), pp. 657-65.

Nachane, D.M. and N. Raje (2007): "Financial Liberalization and Monetary Policy", *Margin—The Journal of Applied Economic Research*, Vol. 1(1), March 2007, pp. 47-83

Narayan, M.K. (2007): Address at the 43rd Munich Conference on Security Policy (11 Feb. 2007).

Obstfeld, M., J. Shambaugh and A. Taylor (2004): "The Trilemma in History: Tradeoffs among Exchange Rates, Monetary Policies and Capital Mobility," *NBER Working Paper No. 10396*.

Plender, J. (1997): *A Stake in the Future: The Stakeholding Solution*, Nicholas Brealey, London.

Quinn, D. (1997): "The correlates of change in international financial regulation", *American Political Science Review*, Vol. 91(3), pp. 531-51.

Rabin, M. and R.H. Thaler (2001): "Anomalies: Risk Aversion", *Journal of Economic Perspectives*, Vol. 15(1), pp. 219-32.

Rakshit, M.K. (2001): "Globalization of capital markets: Some analytical and policy issues" in S. Storm and C. Naastepad (ed.), *Globalization and Economic Development*", Edward Elgar, Cheltenham, UK.

Rangarajan, C. (2000): " Capital flows: Another Look", *Economic and Political Weekly*, Vol. XXXV (50), pp. 4421-27.

Rao, M.J.M and R. Nallari (2001): *Macroeconomic Stabilization and Adjustment*, Oxford University Press, Delhi.

Reddy, Y.V. (2005): *Annual Policy Statement for the Year 2004-05*, Reserve Bank of India.

Reich, R. (1992): *The Work of Nations*, Vintage Books, New York.

Reisen, H. (1996): "Managing volatile capital inflows: The experience of the 1990s", *Asian Development Review*, Vol. 14(1), pp. 47-64.

Reisen, H. and H. Yeches (1993): "Time-varying estimates of the openness of the capital account in Korea and Taiwan", *Journal of Development Economics*, Vol. 4(2), pp. 285-305.

Reserve Bank of India (1997): *Report of the Committee on Capital Account Convertibility (Tarapore I)*.

Reserve Bank of India (2006): *Report of the Committee on Fuller Capital Account Convertibility (Tarapore II)*.

Robinson, W. (1996): *Promoting Polyarchy: Globalization, US Intervention and Hegemony*, Cambridge University Press, Cambridge.

Russel, P.S. and V.M. Torbey (2002): "The efficient market hypothesis on trial: A survey", *Business Quest Journal*, January, pp. 1-19.

Sargent, T. (1982): "The ends of four big inflations" in R. Hall (ed.), *Inflation: Causes and Effects*, University of Chicago Press, Chicago.

Shiller, R.J. (1981): "Do stock prices move too much to be justified by subsequent changes in dividends?", *American Economic Review*, Vol. 71(3), pp. 421-36.

Shleifer, A. and L.H. Summers (1990): "The noise trader approach to finance", *Journal of Economic Perspectives*, Vol. 4(1), pp. 19-33.

Singh, A. (1997): "Liberalization and globalization: An unhealthy euphoria" in J. Michie and J. Grieve-Smith (ed.), *Employment and Economic Performance: Jobs, Inflation and Growth*, Oxford University Press, New York.

Singh, A (2002): "Capital Account Liberalization, Free Long-term Capital Flows, Financial Crises and Economic Development", ESRC Centre for Business Research, University of Cambridge *Working Paper* No. 245.

Spahn, P.B. (1996): "The Tobin tax and exchange rate stability", *Finance and Development*, Vol. 33(2), pp. 24-27.

Stiglitz, J.E. (2000): "Capital market liberalization, economic growth and instability", *World Development*, Vol. 28(6), pp. 1075-86.

Stiglitz, J.E. and A. Weiss (1992): "Asymmetric information in credit markets: Implications for macroeconomic", *Oxford Economic Papers*, Vol. 44(4), pp. 694-724.

Summers, L. (2000): "International Financial Crises: causes, prevention and cures", *American Economic Review Papers and Proceedings*, Vol. 90(2), pp. 1-16.

Summers, L. and V. Summers (1990): "The case for a securities transactions excise tax", *Tax Notes*, (13 August).

Tobin, J. (1978): "A proposal for international monetary reform", *Eastern Economic Journal*, Vol. 4 (July-October), pp. 153-59.

Vegh, C. (1992): "Stopping high inflation: An analytical overview", *IMF Staff Papers,* Vol. 39 (September), pp. 926-95.

Went, R. (2000): "Game, set and match for Mr. Ricardo? The surprising comeback of protectionism in the era of globalized free trade", *Journal of Economic Issues,* Vol. 34(3), pp. 655-77.

Went, R. (2003): "Globalization in the perspective of imperialism", *Science and Society,* Vol. 66(4), pp. 473-97.

Williamson, J. (2006): "Why capital account convertibility in India is premature", *Economic and Political Weekly,* 13 May, pp. 1848-50.

Williamson, J. and Z. Drabek (1999): "Whether and When to Liberalize Capital Account and Financial Services Economic Research and Analysis Division", WTO, *Staff Working Paper No. ERAD-99-03.*

TABLE I

Capital Account Liberalization and Growth

Study	*Number of countries in Sample*	*Openness Measure Used*	*Results*
Quinn 1997	58	Δ(CAL2)	CAC Beneficial for per capita income growth
Klein and Olivei 2000	67	CAL1	CAC Beneficial for per capita income growth if accompanied by financial deepening
Edwards 2001	55	CAL2 and Δ(CAL2)	CAC Beneficial for high-income countries but not for low income countries (in terms of per capita income growth)
Arteta, Eichengreen and Wyplosz 2001	51	CAL2 and Δ(CAL2)	CAC Beneficial if CAL2 is used as liberalization measure
Bekaert, Harvey and Lundblad 2001	30 EMEs	Official dates of stock market liberalization	CAC Beneficial with this measure of liberalization, though most of the benefits are concentrated in the early years.
O'Donell 2001	94	CAL1 and Volume	CAC Beneficial if Volume is used as liberalization measure, but not with CAL1
Grilli and Milesi-Ferretti 1995	61	CAL1	No evidence for CAC being Beneficial for per capita economic growth
Rodrik 1998	100	CAL1	No evidence for CAC being Beneficial for per capita economic growth
Kraay 1998	117	CAL1, Volume and CAL2	CAC Beneficial if Volume is used as liberalization measure, but not with CAL1 or CAL2
Edison *et al.* 2002	89	CAL1, CAL2 and Dates of stock market liberalization	CAC Beneficial for high-income but not for developing economies countries and East Asian economies

Notes: Δ(CAL2) represents changes in CAL2, Volume refers to the volume of capital inflows.

TABLE 2

Countrywise Share of Average Daily Forex Market Turnover (as of 2004)

Country	*Share*
UK	31.3%
US	19.2%
Japan	8.3%
Singapore	5.2%
Germany	4.9%
Hong Kong	4.2%
Australia	3.4%
Switzerland	3.3%
France	2.7%
Canada	2.2%
Others	15.3%
Total	100%

Source: BIS: *Triennial Central Bank Survey of Foreign Exchange and Derivatives Market Activity, 2005.*

TABLE 3

Cross-Currency Share of Trade (as of 2004)

	US$	*Euro*	*Japanese Yen*	*British Sterling*	*Swiss Franc*	*Australian $*	*Canadian $*	*New Zealand $*
US $	—	28%	17%	14%	4%	5%	4%	—
Euro		—	3%	2%	1%	—	—	—
Japanese Yen			—	—	—	—	—	—
British Sterling				—	—	—	—	—
Swiss Franc					—	—	—	—
Australian $						—	—	—
Canadian $							—	—
New Zealand $								—

Source: Same as Table 2.

Table 4

Capital Inflows into India (US $ Billion)

	2001-02	2002-03	2003-04	2004-05	2005-06 (P)
A. Foreign Direct Investment (I+II+III)	**6130**	**5035**	**4322**	**6051**	**7752**
I. Equity (a+b+c+d+e)	4095	2764	2229	3778	5820
a. Government	2221	919	928	1062	1126
b. RBI	767	739	534	1258	2233
c. NRI	35	—	—	—	—
d. Acquisition of Shares	881	916	735	930	2181
e. Equity capital of Unincorporated Bodies	191	190	32	528	280
II. Reinvested Earnings	1645	1833	1460	1904	1676
III. Other Capital	390	438	633	369	256
B. Foreign Portfolio Investment (a+b+c)	**2021**	**979**	**11377**	**9315**	**12492**
a. GDRs/ADRs	477	600	459	613	2552
b. FIIs	1505	377	10918	8686	9926
c. Offshore Funds and others	39	2	-	16	14
Total Investment (A+B)	**8151**	**6014**	**15699**	**15366**	**20244**

Table 5

Preconditions for Capital A/C Liberalization (Tarapore I)

Item	*Precondition*	*Position (2005-06)*
Gross Fiscal Deficit (as % of GDP)	<3.5%	4.1%
Inflation	3% to 5% (3-year average)	4.6% (3-year average)
Gross NPAs (as % of total advances)	<5%	5.2% (as of 2004-05)
Average effective CRR	3.0%	5.0%
Current A/c deficit (as % of GDP)	<2.0%	>3.0%
Debt servicing ratio	<20%	10.2%
Forex reserves	>6 months Imports cover	11.6 months Imports cover

TABLE 6

Implementation of Recommendations of Tarapore Committee I

	Recommendations	*Action Taken*
1.	Direct Investment in foreign ventures by Indian corporates be allowed upto $50 million at level of authorized dealer (anything above this limit to be routed through a special committee)	This limit currently stands at $100 million
2.	Corporates be permitted to open offices abroad	Implemented
3.	Restrictions on end-use of ECBs (external commercial borrowings) for rupee expenditures be removed	Implemented
4.	Exporters be allowed to retain 100% of forex earnings in foreign currency accounts.	Implemented
5.	Direct portfolio investment by non-residents be allowed (on the same footing as FIIs and NRIs)	Disallowed
6.	Banks be allowed to borrow in overseas markets and to deploy funds outside India	Largely implemented
7.	Individuals be allowed to invest in markets abroad to the extent of $25,000	Implemented
8.	Residents be allowed to have foreign currency denominated deposits with corporates and banks	Allowed but subject to some restrictions.

2

Capital Account Convertibility in India: A Review

Biswajit Chatterjee and Ram Pratap Sinha

Abstract

Since the eighties, many developing countries started to liberalize their capital accounts from the belief that the greater access to international capital markets would lower their cost of capital and promote economic growth. The euphoria on capital account liberalization was, however, short-lived, as many of the Asian and Latin American emerging market economies experienced severe currency and banking crises in the 1990s.Quite a number of the countries re-imposed some form of capital control in order to cope with the crisis. In this backdrop, the present paper makes a survey of the capital account liberalization process in India and examines the possible consequences of capital account opening up in India.

INTRODUCTION

Currency convertibility refers to the right/freedom to convert the domestic currency into other internationally accepted currencies and *vice versa*. Convertibility, however, has two dimensions: (i) current account convertibility and (ii) capital account convertibility. Current account convertibility refers to the freedom in respect of payments and transfers for current international transactions. Capital account convertibility, on the other hand, implies freedom of currency conversion in relation to capital transactions in terms of inflows and outflows. Capital account convertibility may thus be seen as an integral part of the financial openness of the country.

Historically, countries used to have different forms of restrictions on international movement of capital. Article VIII of the International Monetary Fund (IMF) puts an obligation on a member to avoid imposing restrictions on the making of payments and transfers for current international transactions. Members may co-operate for the purpose of making the exchange control regulations of members more effective. Article VI(3), however, allows members to exercise such controls as are necessary to regulate international capital movements, but not so as to restrict payments for current transactions or which would unduly delay transfers of funds in settlement of commitments.

Since the eighties, many developing countries started to liberalize their capital accounts from the belief that the greater access to international capital markets would lower their cost of capital and promote economic growth. The process gained further momentum in the nineties so much so that the International Monetary Fund was about to amend the articles of agreement to incorporate capital account convertibility as one of the obligations of Fund membership. The euphoria on capital account liberalization was, however, short-lived, as many of the Asia and Latin American emerging market economies experienced severe currency and banking crises in the 1990s. Quite a number of the countries re-imposed some form of capital control in order to cope with the crisis. The costs and benefits or risks and gains from capital account liberalization or controls are still being debated within academic and policy-making circles. The IMF, which had floated the idea of changing its Charter to include capital account liberalization in its mandate, shelved this proposal.

The Scope of the Present Paper

Since the introduction of economic reforms, capital account has been partially opened in India in a gradual and controlled fashion. In the recent past, however, the government has declared its intention (in more than one ways) to introduce capital account convertibility in a more comprehensive manner. In particular, two Committees were set up by the Ministry of Finance in 2004 and 2005 to examine the possibility of liberalizing FII investment in India. Further, in 2006, the *RBI* had set the Committee on Fuller Capital Account . Convertibility which had also sent its recommendations.

Given this backdrop, the present paper makes a survey of the capital account liberalization process in India and examines the possible consequences of capital account opening up in India. The paper is divided into three sections. Section 1 provides a brief review cross-country experience regarding capital account liberalization and section 2 provides an outline of the Indian scenario. Section 3 deals with the two committee reports relating to capital account convertibility. Finally, section 4 examines the macroeconomic implications of capital account liberalization.

SECTION I

EVOLUTION OF CAPITAL ACCOUNT OPENNESS: THE GLOBAL EXPERIENCE

Till the outbreak of the World War I, the developed countries followed a policy of laissez faire, with no capital controls. This period was characterized by a boom in international flows of goods, labour and capital across nations. Most of the foreign investment during this period was of long-term nature and was mainly directed towards the creation of infrastructure, especially utilities and railroads. The phase ended with the onset of the First World War I. After the conclusion of the war there was a transient revival of capital movement which again subsided because of the onset of the Great Depression.

After the World War II, both developed and developing

countries maintained tight control over capital movement as this was considered as an integral part of the Bretton Woods system. This phase of capital account control continued upto the seventies. The Bretton Woods system however collapsed in the mid-seventies and this caused policy reversal for the developed countries and some of the developing countries in the matter of capital account control. There has been a general shift towards capital account liberalization which coincided with the adoption of market-oriented economic policies (see Table 1 for the information about the adoption of capital account liberalization in developed countries).

TABLE I

Capital Account Liberalization in Developed Countries

Country	*Year*
United States	1974
United Kingdom	1979
Germany	1981
Netherlands	1986
Denmark	1988
France	1990
Sweden	1989
Italy	1990
Belgium	1990
Austria	1991
Finland	1991
Spain	1992
Ireland	1993
Greece	1994
Japan	1991
Australia	1985
New Zealand	1985

Source: Bakker, Age and Bryan Chapple (2002), 'Advanced Country Experiences with Capital Account Liberalisation', *IMF Occasional Paper No. 214*, IMF, Washington D.C.

In the early eighties many Asian/Latin American economies initiated capital account liberalization. There was a general orientation towards opening the capital account and in a world fast integrating through both trade and financial flows, capital controls were considered as ineffective and even distortionary. Consequently, the volume of capital flows into the developing economies accelerated till the mid-1990s. The general fear associated with capital account openness has been the outflow of capital, but the opposite has also been true for certain economies. Soon the magnitude of capital flows became unmanageable for the developing economies and sterilisation operations became increasingly ineffective. Under the circumstances some of the developing countries imposed restrictions on capital movement across the border. While some economies faced the challenge of managing increased inflows, some others experienced reversal of flows which led to a series of crises during the mid-1990s.

Section 2

CAPITAL ACCOUNT LIBERALISATION IN INDIA— A BRIEF REVIEW

Upto the eighties, India largely followed a path of self-reliance with strict control over cross-border capital movements .Since 1991, however, there has been a gradual but steady shift in favour of capital account openness.

Liberalization of Foreign Direct Investment

Since 1991, the regulatory framework for capital inflows in India has been significantly liberalised particularly for FDI and portfolio flows (mostly FIIs). Excepting six prohibited sectors, other sectors have been opened up for foreign direct investments. However, in certain sectors like insurance, banking and telecommunications the FDI limit is below 50%. Between 1990-91 and 2005-06, cumulative FDI in India amounted to US $ 41,519 million (Table 2).

Liberalization of Foreign Institutional Investment

On 14th September 1992, FIIs were first permitted to

TABLE 2

Foreign Investment Inflows into India (In Million US $)

Year	*Direct Investment*	*Portfolio Investment*	*Total*
1990-91	97	6	103
1991-92	129	4	133
1992-93	315	244	559
1993-94	586	3567	4153
1994-95	1314	3824	5138
1995-96	2144	2748	4892
1996-97	2821	3312	6133
1997-98	3557	1828	5385
1998-99	2462	-61	2401
1999-00	2155	3026	5181
2000-01	4029	2760	6789
2001-02	6130	2021	8151
2002-03	5035	979	6014
2003-04	4322	11377	15699
2004-05	5652	9315	14967
2005-06	7751	12492	20243

Source: RBI (2006): *Handbook of Statistics on Indian Economy,* www.rbi.org.in.

invest in the securities traded on the primary and secondary security markets, including shares/debentures/warrants of listed companies and units of mutual funds. Between 1993-94 and 2004-05, the number of FIIs registered in India increased from 3 to 685 (see Table 3). FIIs registered with SEBI are of two types:

(a) *Regular FIIs*: They are required to invest not less than 70% of their investments in equity-related instruments and up to 30% in non-equity instruments.

(b) *Debt Fund FIIs*: They are permitted to invest only in debt instruments.

FII investment is, however, permitted subject to the following exposure limits:

(a) Total exposure in a company by a single FII is limited to 10%.
(b) Total exposure by (all) FIIs to a company is limited to 49% under the special procedure scheme.
(c) There are specific sectoral caps in respect of sectoral caps in respect of sectors like banking, insurance, telecom services, media, etc.
(d) FII investment in the debt market is capped at $1.5 billion for corporate bonds and $2 billion in respect of government securities.

Access to Overseas Capital Markets

Indian companies are permitted to raise equity capital from overseas capital markets through American/Global Depository Receipts. Further, they can make use of the ECB/FCCB route for borrowings up to $500 million. They can also invest overseas through the ODI (Overseas Direct Investment) Route excepting in sectors like real estate or banking.

TABLE 3

FII Presence in India (1992-93 to 2004-05)

Year	*No of FIIs Registered at The Year End*	*Net FII Investment. During the Year (US$ Million)*
1992-93	0	1
1993-94	3	1665
1994-95	156	1503
1995-96	353	2009
1996-97	439	1926
1997-98	496	979
1998-99	450	-390
1999-00	506	2135
2000-01	528	1847
2001-02	490	1505
2002-03	502	377
2003-04	540	10918
2004-05	685	8279

Source: Ministry of Finance (2005): *Report of the Expert Group on Encouraging FII Flows and Checking The Vulnerability of Capital Markets to Speculative Flows, www.finmin.nic.in.*

SECTION 3

TOWARDS FULLER CAPITAL ACCOUNT CONVERTIBILITY IN INDIA

A distinguishing feature of the capital account liberalization process in India has been the absence of a level playing field for all sections of the population with regard to capital outflows/inflows. The capital account was tightly controlled for the resident Indians. Especially, there was a total ban on capital outflows For resident corporates, inflows were allowed subject to a complex set of approvals and procedures. For outflows from the corporate sector, some very limited facilities were provided but, again, subject to several approval requirements and procedural hurdles. Banks had very limited facilities for borrowing abroad although they were allowed to raise resources abroad outside the very restricted limits for purposes of financing exports and raising of deposits under the NR(E)RA and FCNR(B) Schemes. Capital account convertibility had all along been available for non-residents. However, within the non-residents category, the non-resident Indians (NRIs) enjoyed special privileges.

The Committee on Capital Account Convertibility (1997)

The Committee on Capital Account Convertibility (1997) was set up by the RBI under the Chairmanship of S.S. Tarapore, former Deputy Governor of the RBI. The major terms of reference of the Committee were as follows:

(i) To recommend measures for achieving full capital account convertibility in India,

(ii) To specify sequencing and timing of capital account liberalisation measures, and

(iii) To suggest domestic policy measures with the specified sequencing.

The Committee in its Report (submitted in May 1997) had set out detailed preconditions for moving towards capital account convertibility and also set out the timing and sequencing of liberalization measures. In particular, the

Committee suggested that the implementation of capital account convertibility be spread over a three year period 1997-2000. Further, attainment of a mandated inflation rate of 3% was considered as a crucial precondition by the Committee. In addition to the conduct exchange rate policy and the adequacy of foreign exchange reserve are to be reviewed on a regular basis.

In this context the Committee recommended that:

(a) The mandated rate of inflation for the period 1997-2000 should be about 3-5 per cent;
(b) The exchange rate should be targeted within +/- 5 per cent of the neutral Real Effective Exchange Rate (REER), and
(c) Foreign exchange reserves should not be less than six months of imports over the period 1997-2000.

Table 4 compares the preconditions set out by the 1997 Committee with the actual position in 2005-06.

TABLE 4

Preconditions for CAC in India: Tarapore I *Vs.* Actuals

Item	*Recommendation of Tarapore Committee-I (1997) for 1999-2000*	*Actual Position in 2005-06*
Gross Fiscal Deficit (GFD) of the Central Govt. as a % of GDP	3.5	4.1
The Rate of Inflation	3.0 -5.0 (average for 3 years)	4.6 (average for 3 years)
Financial Sector		
(i) Gross NPAs as a percentage of total advances	5.0	5.2 (2004-05)
(ii) Average effective Cash Reserve Ratio for the banking system	3.0	5.0

Source: RBI (2006): *Report of the Committee on Fuller Capital Account Convertibility*, www.rbi.org.in

Sustainability of CAC (1997) Proposals

Rao (1997) considered the sustainability of the Tarapore I recommendations in the context of a theoretical framework which explored the interactions between money, inflation, reserves, interest rates and growth. The analysis showed that full financial openness requires not only mutually consistent monetary and exchange rate policies but also policy sustainability in order to prevent speculative attacks on currency followed by a run on foreign currency reserves. Rao further found that a 6 per cent growth rate and a 5 percent rate of inflation are mutually inconsistent with the recommended reserve requirements. However, they are sustainable under the current structure of foreign interest rates, although it will be essential to pursue a tight money policy to make them sustainable. The sustainable growth rate and the rate of inflation are negatively and positively related to the world interest rate. Rao commented that the wide band suggested by Tarapore I for monitoring the real exchange rate is undesirable and he suggested a band of +/-1 per cent to prevent speculative attacks.

Opening of the Capital Account Since 1997

The RBI has taken action on a number of recommendations suggested by the Committee on CAC (1997) but the extent of implementation has been somewhat muted on some of the proposed measures (e.g., outflows by resident individuals and overseas borrowing by banks), while for some other measures, the RBI has proceeded far beyond the Committee's recommendations (e.g. outflows by resident corporates). RBI has, however, taken a number of additional measures outside the 1997 Committee's recommendations.

Most of the capital account liberalization measures proposed by the 1997 Committee were essentially in relation to residents. While resident corporates have been provided fairly liberal limits, the liberalization for resident individuals has been hesitant and in some cases inoperative because of procedural impediments. The RBI has liberalized the framework on an *ad hoc* basis. Progressively, as capital account liberalization gathers momentum, it is essential that there should be a rationalisation/simplification of the regulatory system and procedures in a manner wherein there can be a viable and meaningful monitoring of the capital flows.

TABLE 5

Implementation of the Committee on CAC (1997) Recommendations: Position as on April 2006

Category	*No. of items listed in recom-mendations*	*Nos. Partly Imple-mented*	*Nos. Fully Imple-mented*	*Total*	*Items not Imple-mented*	*Additional Measures by RBI*
Corporates (R)	10	4	4	8	2	9
Corporates (NR)	3	2	1	3	0	3
Banks (R)	6	4	1	5	1	3
Banks (NR)	1	1	-	1	-	-
Non-Banks (R)	2	-	1	1	1	1
Non-Banks (NR) FIIs	4	1	3	4	0	1
Individuals (R)	3	2	-	2	1	3
Individuals (NR)	4	1	3	4	0	3
Financial Markets	7	4	2	6	1	-
Total	40	19	15	34	6	23

Source: RBI (2006): *Report of The Committee on Fuller Capital Account Convertibility*, www.rbi.org.in

The Committee on Capital Account Convertibility (2006)

In 2006, the Reserve Bank of India (RBI), in consultation with the Government of India, appointed, on March 20, 2006, a Committee to set out the Roadmap Towards Fuller Capital Account Convertibility under the Chairmanship of Shri S.S. Tarapore. The reasons for having a second committee on the same issue are mainly as under:

(i) The 1997 Committee's framework related to the three year period ending in March 2000 while the current assessment has been undertaken six years after the last year in the Committee's time frame for measures.

(ii) Secondly, the Indian macroeconomic situation as also the international economy have undergone significant changes since 1997.

(iii) Thirdly, there have been large capital inflows into India in recent years and much of the authorities' efforts have been directed towards handling these large capital flows in terms of the domestic monetary expansion and evolving of suitable neutralisation policies.

(iv) Capital account convertibility has to be viewed as an ongoing process with the gradual entrenchment of the preconditions/signposts and the implementation of measures.

The terms of reference of the 2nd Committee were as under:

(i) To review the experience of various measures of capital account liberalisation in India since the beginning of the process of economic reform,

(ii) To examine implications of fuller capital account convertibility on monetary and exchange rate management, financial markets and financial system,

(iii) To study the implications of dollarisation in India of domestic assets and liabilities and internationalisation of the Indian rupee,

(iv) To provide a comprehensive medium-term operational framework, with sequencing and timing, for fuller capital account convertibility taking into account the above implications and progress in fiscal management of both centre and states,

(v) To survey regulatory framework in countries which have advanced towards fuller capital account convertibility,

(vi) To recommend appropriate policy measures and prudential safeguards to ensure monetary and financial stability, and

(vii) To make such other recommendations as the Committee may deem relevant to the subject.

Recommendations of The Committee on Capital Account Convertibility 2006

The Committee on CAC (2006) recommended that there should be an early rationalization/consolidation of the various capital account liberalization facilities. Furthermore, it is observed that with the formal adoption of current account convertibility in 1994 and the subsequent gradual liberalization of the capital account, some inconsistencies in the policy framework have emerged and the Committee recommends that these issues should be comprehensively examined by the RBI. The major measures proposed by the Committee on CAC (2006) relate to the liberalization for capital outflows by corporates and individuals. As regards inflows by the non-resident, the Committee has recommended that NR and NRIs should be treated on a uniform basis. *Inter alia,* the following are the major recommendations of the Committee:

(i) Level Playing Fields for All Categories of Non-Residents

The Committee pointed out that movement towards fuller CAC implies that all non-residents (corporates and individuals) should be treated equally. This would mean the removal of the tax benefits presently accorded to NRIs via special bank deposit schemes for NRIs, viz., Non-Resident External Rupee Account [NR(E)RA] and Foreign Currency Non-Resident (Banks) Scheme [FCNR(B)]. The Committee thus recommended that the present tax benefit for these special deposit schemes for NRIs, should be reviewed by the government. On the other hand, in the case of the present NRI schemes for various types of investments, other than deposits, there are a number of procedural hurdles and these should be examined by the Government and the RBI.

(ii) Capital Account Liberalisation for Resident Indians

In the present circumstances, the capital restrictions are clearly more stringent for the resident Indians than for non-residents. Furthermore, resident corporates face a relatively more liberal regime than resident individuals. Till recently, resident individuals faced a virtual ban on capital outflow but a small relaxation has been undertaken in the recent period. The Committee decided in favour of some liberalization in the rules governing resident individuals investing abroad for the purpose of asset diversification. It would also be desirable to consider a gradual liberalization for resident corporates/business entities, banks, non-banks and individuals.

(iii) Review of Discriminatory Tax Treaties

With the introduction of fuller capital account convertibility, the issue of investments being channelled through a particular country so as to obtain tax benefits would come to the fore as investments through other channels get discriminated against. Such discriminatory tax treaties are not consistent with an increasing liberalization of the capital account as distortions inevitably emerge, possibly raising the cost of capital to the host country. With global integration of capital markets, tax policies should be harmonised. It would, therefore, be desirable that the government undertakes a review of tax policies and tax treaties.

(iv) Composition of Capital Inflow

The Committee emphasised on setting out a hierarchy of preferences relating to the liberalization of capital inflows. Thus rupee denominated debt which would be preferable to foreign currency debt, medium and long-term debt in preference to short-term debt, and direct investment to portfolio flows. There is a need to monitor the amount of short-term borrowings and banking capital, both of which have been shown to be problematic during the crisis in East Asia and in other developing economies.

(v) Strengthening of the Risk Management Framework of Commercial Banks

Greater focus may be needed on regulatory and supervisory issues in banking to strengthen the entire risk management framework. Preference should be given to control volatility in cross-border capital flows in prudential policy measures. Given the importance that the commercial banks occupy in the Indian financial system, the banking system should be the focal point for appropriate prudential policy measures. In the absence of strong risk management policies and treasury management skills, banks may be inclined to take excessive risk. Strong prudential policies (applicable to both balance sheet items as also off-balance sheet items) will help banks in minimising financial risks and possible losses.

The Time Frame for the Implementation of Fuller Capital Account Convertibility

The Committee (2006) recommended a broad time frame of a five year period in three phases, 2006-07 (Phase I), 2007-08 and 2008-09 (Phase II) and 2009-10 and 2010-11 (Phase III) with a review to be done after the completion of each Phase before moving on to the next Phase. The roadmap so recommended is to be considered as a broad time-path for measures and the pace of actual implementation would depend on the authorities' assessment of overall macroeconomic developments and specific problems encountered (if any). The Committee recommended that at the end of the five-year period, ending in 2010-11, there should be a comprehensive review to chalk out the future course of action.

SECTION 4

MACRO-ECONOMIC IMPLICATIONS OF CAPITAL ACCOUNT CONVERTIBILITY

The standard arguments put forward in favour of capital account convertibility are based on the principles of efficiency maximization derived in the context of a neo-classical framework. The major arguments advanced in this connection are as under:

(a) If capital account is opened up, capital will flow to the location where it earns the highest rate of return. The investors of capital can higher rate of return by making global allocation of the resources which is not possible under capital account restrictions. This has also the accompanying diversification benefits as investors returns are not significantly affected by market downturn in one country.

(b) The inflow of foreign capital enables the recipient countries to bridge saving-investment and foreign exchange gaps. The reduction in cost of capital also promotes investment in the economy in the economy and facilitate relative (if not absolute) convergence in growth rates.

(c) Capital account openness compels the capital scarce countries to frame legislation which are investor friendly which in turn promotes investment and growth. Capital account liberalization also provides shock absorbers in the sense that during a macro-economic downturn, lower wages will attract foreign capital and generate counter-cyclical movements. For further details, see Stiglitz (2000).

Capital Account Convertibility and Economic Growth: Empirical Evidence

There are very few studies connecting capital account convertibility and economic growth. Rodrik (1998),on the basis of a sample of nearly 100 countries for the period 1975-89, tried to see the association of capital account liberalization with three indicators of economic performance: per capita GDP growth, investment(as a % of GDP) and the rate of inflation. He found no association between capital account liberalisation and long-term economic performance of the respective countries

Capital account convertibility, on the other hand, has facilitated the recurrence of financial sector crises in the emerging market economies (see Table 7).

Why Does Capital Account Liberalization Generate Problems?

Experience of the affected countries suggest that the risks of capital account convertibility arise mostly from the following sources:

TABLE 6

Developing Countries with Capital Account Openness (1973-96)

Country	*Period*
Argentina	1994-96
Bolivia	1987-96
Costa Rica	1973-74, 1981-82, 1996
Ecuador	1973-93
Gambia	1992-96
Guatemala	1974-80, 1990-96
Honduras	1973-80
Hong Kong	1973-96
Indonesia	1973-96
Iran	1975-78
Liberia	1973-84
Malaysia	1974-96
Mexico	1973-82
Nicaragua	1973-78
Niger	1996
Panama	1973-96
Paraguay	1983-84
Peru	1979-84, 1994-96
Seychelles	1978-96
Singapore	1979-96
Togo	1995
Uruguay	1979-93
Republic of Yemen	1973-90

Source: Kim (1997): *Does Capital Account Liberalization Discipline Budget Deficits?*, Harvard University, 1997.

(a) Problems with Exchange Rate Management

Most currency crises arise out of prolonged overvalued exchange rates, leading to unsustainable current account deficits. An excessive appreciation of the exchange rate causes exporting industries to become unviable, and imports to become much more competitive, causing the current account deficit to worsen. Further, in a floating exchange rate regime, with uncertainties attached to exchange rates, interest rates are not equalized across the border. Evidences

TABLE 7

Episodes of Currency Crises in Emerging Market Economies

Region	*Period*
Mexico	1994-95
East Asia (including Thailand, Malaysia, Indonesia, South Korea and The Philippines)	1997-98
Brazil	1998
Russia	1998
Argentina	1998-2001

Source: Various IMF Documents.

regarding divergence of real rates of return can be obtained in Frankel (1993).Even countries that had apparently comfortable fiscal positions, have experienced currency crises and rapid deterioration of the exchange rate. In many other economies, large unsustainable levels of external and domestic debt directly led to currency crises. Hence, a transparent fiscal consolidation is essential, to reduce the risk of currency crisis.

(b) Procyclicality of Capital Inflow

Empirical evidences suggest that capital account convertibility promotes instability. This is because capital inflows are inherently pro-cyclical as the ordinary global investor exhibits herd behaviour. The financial markets are thus fundamentally different from commodity market.

(c) Short-term Borrowings

Opening up of foreign investment in domestic debt market (especially the issuance of foreign currency linked domestic bonds) is a major facilitator of currency crises. This is because, short-term debt flows react quickly and adversely during currency crises. During a financial crises, receivables are typically postponed, and payables accelerated, aggravating the balance of payments position.

(d) Weakness of the Financial Sector

Domestic financial institutions (particularly commercial banks) need to be strong and resilient. As the cross-border exposure grows with capital account liberalization, it is essential to monitor carefully the quality of balance sheets in terms of risk exposure (with regard to on and off balance sheet items). The quality and proactive nature of market regulation is also critical to the success of efficient functioning of financial markets during times of currency crises.

Capital Account Openness: The Indian Experience So Far

(a) Behaviour of FII Investment

India has performed relatively well during the previous episodes of emerging market failures. Table 8 shows the behaviour of BSE Index and FII capital inflow during the East Asian crises. The main reason behind this was the fact that FII investments occupied a small part of the Indian equity market.

TABLE 8

Capital Market Behaviour in India During The East Asian Crises (1997-98)

Month	*BSE Index for the Month*	*FII Investments (Rs. crore)*
July 1997	4256.11	1002.8
August 1997	4276.31	493.66
September 1997	3944.78	598.59
October 1997	3991.75	641.59
November 1997	3611.83	-289.87
December 1997	3515.54	-182.38
January 1997	3472.87	-374.97
February 1997	3402.96	629.05
March 1997	3816.89	472.22

Source: Ministry of Finance (2005): *Report of The Expert Group On Encouraging FII Flows and Checking The Vulnerability of Capital Markets to Speculative Flows*, www.finmin.nic.in.

Chakraborty (2001) found that the FII net inflows in to India were related to the return available from the Indian equity market. The same result is obtained from the study of Mukherjee, Bose and Coondoo (2002). This is contrary to the general perception that FII activities in India have a strong demonstration effect and thus is a key driver of the domestic market performance. Gordon and Gupta (2003), however, found that both global and domestic factors are important in determining portfolio flows. The key determining factors include the London Inter-Bank Offer Rate (LIBOR), lagged stock market returns, rating downgrades and exchange rate behaviour of the rupee.

FII investments account for around 12 per cent of the spot market volumes. Further, they account for approximately 5.1 per cent of the monthly turnover in the derivatives market. In respect of the cumulative open position in single stock futures, the contribution of FII is 25 per cent. In the recent past FII inflows have shown stability and growth mainly on account of the following factors:

(a) strong economic fundamentals and attractive valuation of the corporate sector,
(b) on set of prudential regulatory standards including efficient clearing, settlement and risk management systems and high quality disclosure and corporate governance practices, and
(c) Strengthening of the rupee *vis-a-vis* the US dollar.

(b) Monetary Management

The structural changes in the Indian financial system have resulted in the growing importance of the rate channels as compared to the quantum channels. The Working Group on Money Supply (1998) indicated that output response to expansionary monetary policy operating through the interest rate was found to be stronger and more persistent than that of the credit channel. On the other hand, the monetary transmission process in respect of inflation was found to be stronger through interest rate than the exchange rate, given the low degree of openness of the economy.

In view of the structural changes in the Indian financial

system, the RBI in recent times has adopted the Multiple Indicator Approach whereby policy formulation is done on the basis of information in respect of a host of quantum and rate variables including yields in money, capital and gilt markets, trends in inflation, expansion of credit by banks and financial institutions, foreign exchange position, fiscal position, international trade and trends in national output.

In the changed circumstances, the RBI now makes increasing use of the bank rate and the repo rate. The conduct of sterilization operation (involving an exchange of foreign currency asset for domestic currency assets) in the Indian context is quite important for neutralizing the impact of capital inflows. Kohli (2001) emphasised on the need to have an in-depth study of the quasi-fiscal and other costs of sterilization operation. Table 9 shows the growth in M_0 and M_3 and the accumulation of foreign exchange asset by the banking sector.

TABLE 9

Money Supply Composition with Partial Capital Account Liberalization

(Figures in Rs. crore)

Year	M_0	M_3	*Net Foreign Exchange Asset of the RBI*	*Net Foreign Exchange Asset of the RBI*
1990-91	87779	265828	7983	2598
1991-92	99505	317049	18838	2388
1992-93	110779	364016	22647	1796
1993-94	138672	431084	51422	3190
1994-95	169283	527596	74220	4312
1995-96	194457	599191	74092	8049
1996-97	199985	696012	94817	10679
1997-98	226402	821332	115890	22204
1998-99	259286	980960	137954	39900
1999-00	280555	1124174	165880	39768
2000-01	303311	1313220	197175	52645
2001-02	337970	1498355	263969	47066
2002-03	369061	17117960	358244	35471
2003-04	436512	2251449	484413	42173
2004-05	489135	2729535	612790	36465

Source: RBI(2005): *Handbook of Statistics on the Indian Economy*, www.rbi.org.in.

The Committee on FCAC (2006) has emphasised on the mutual compatibility of the sterilisationt operations and interventions in the foreign exchange markets. In this connection, the Committee has made the following recommendations:

(i) Interest Rate Targeting

With greater integration of domestic and international markets, the RBI should progressively give more weightage to international real interest rates so that the Indian real interest rates are aligned with international real interest rates. Any mismatch between short-term and long-term interest rates could be corrected through appropriate open market operations Further, interest rate changes should be small enough to avoid large capital inflow or outflow which can be destabilizing for the economy.

(ii) Amendment in the SLR Legislation

While the RBI (on the basis of the recommendations of The Working Group on Money Supply (1998)) is gradually moving away from monetary targeting, the Committee on FCAC felt that it would be necessary to continue to actively use the instrument of reserve requirements for the time being. Thus the RBI should have the flexibility to change the Statutory Liquidity Ratio (SLR) below 25 per cent as and when necessary.

(iii) Modifications in LAF Operations

Within a span of six years, the Liquidity Adjustment Facility (LAF) has become an effective instrument. The repo and reverse repo interest rates are key signalling rates in the system. The Committee on FCAC has recommended that the LAF should be essentially an instrument of equilibrating very short-term liquidity and that the RBI should greater freedom in operating the LAF. Under the present system of fixed rate repo/reverse repo auctions, these rates become a major policy announcement and this restricts the degree of freedom the RBI needs in its day-to-day operations. The RBI should activate variable rate repo/reverse repo auctions or repo/reverse repo operations on a real time basis. The RBI should also make use of SLR and CRR as supportive instruments.

(iv) Management of Excess Liquidity

In order to cope with excess liquidity problem arising out of high levels of FII inflows, the Committee on FCAC recommended (under exceptional circumstances) the imposition of an unremunerated reserve requirement on fresh FII inflows using the FEMA Rules for FIIs. In such a system, FIIs would be required to retain a stipulated percentage of the inflows with the bank and the bank in turn would be required to transfer these balances to the RBI. The impounded balance would be released to FIIs after a stipulated period. Such a measure, should however, be used as a temporary measure only for a few months.

(c) Management of the Exchange Rate

Table 10 shows the behaviour of the Indian rupee *vis-a-vis* other currencies during the reform period. The two measures of exchange rate REER (Real Effective Exchange

TABLE 10

Annual Average Indices of the Indian Rupee (REER and NEER)

Year	*REER-Export-based Weights*	*NEER-Export-based Weights*	*REER-Trade-based Weights*	*NEER-Trade-based Weights*
1993	100.08	99.62	100.08	99.61
1994	103.60	99.30	103.31	99.86
1995	102.61	93.41	100.97	94.07
1996	97.55	88.16	95.41	88.42
1997	102.61	91.72	100.36	91.85
1998	96.36	90.23	94.52	89.11
1999	94.85	90.58	95.29	90.89
2000	98.07	90.57	99.30	92.19
2001	98.90	89.25	100.88	91.52
2002	96.40	87.57	98.90	90.08
2003	98.17	87.68	99.04	87.60
2004	98.28	87.87	99.68	86.83
2005	100.57	90.74	102.27	89.39

Source: RBI (2005): *Handbook of Statistics on the Indian Economy*, www.rbi.org.in.

Rate) and NEER (Nominal Effective Exchange Rate) are based on 36-currency bilateral weights. Note that REER indices have been recalculated from April 1993 onwards using the new Wholesale Price Index Series (Base: 1993-94=100). A new 36-currency REER/NEER series has been introduced from December 2005 onwards.

Exchange rate management, in the context of capital account openness, is a dicey proposition. On the one hand, large capital inflows could result in appreciation of the exchange rate and a loss of international competitiveness. On the other hand, large capital outflows could result in sharp depreciation of the currency with the associated inflationary impacts. The implementation of the exchange rate policy gave the Committee on FCAC some concern. The IMF has classified the Indian exchange rate regime as a "managed float with no predetermined path for the exchange rate". So far the RBI has put emphasis on volatility management. The Committee on FCAC has emphasised on the level of the exchange rate also as sharp appreciation/depreciation of the exchange rate in real effective terms can have adverse impacts on the economy.

Towards Fuller Capital Account Convertibility: The Concluding Remarks

India has so far managed its regime of partial capital account openness quite well. The big question, however, is: Will India be able to insulate its capital market from negative shocks in future when FII investment will be much more significant? Further, in almost every country the implementation of capital account convertibility led to an appreciation of the exchange rate of the domestic currency which acted as a catalyst to financial crises. The Committee on Fuller Capital Account Convertibility (2006) commented: 'While the impossibility of the trinity (fixed exchange rate, open capital account and independent monetary policy) may be a theoretical construct, in practice, it is possible to approach situations, which are close enough, through a combination of prudential policies.' Only future can tell us whether India will succeed in doing so.

REFERENCES

Bakker, Age and Bryan Chapple (2002): "Advanced Country Experiences with Capital Account Liberalisation," *IMF Occasional* Paper No. 214, IMF, Washington D.C.

Chakraborty, R. (2001): "FII Flows to India: Nature and Causes", *Money and Finance*, Volume 2 No 7, October-December 2001.

Frankel, S. (1993): "International Financial Integration: Relations Between Interest Rates and Exchange Rates" in D. Das (ed.), *'International Finance: Contemporary Issues'*, Routledge, London.

Gordon, J. and P. Gupta (2003): "Portfolio Flows in to India: Do Domestic Fundamentals Matter?", *IMF Working Paper* No 03/20, January 2003, International Monetary Fund, Washington DC.

Kim, W. (1997): *Does Capital Account Liberalisation Discipline Budget Deficits*, Harvard University, 1997.

Kohli, R. (2001): "Capital Account Liberalisation—Empirical Evidence and Policy Issues-II," *Economic and Political Weekly*, April 21, 2001.

Ministry of Finance (2005): *Report of the Expert Group on Encouraging FII Flows and Checking the Vulnerability of Capital Markets to Speculative Flows*, www.finmin.nic.in.

Ministry of Finance (2004): *Report of the Committee on Encouraging Liberalisation of Foreign Institutional Investment*, www.finmin.nic.in.

Mukherjee P., S. Bose and D. Coondoo (2002): "Foreign Institutional Investment in the Daily Flows During January 1999-May 2002," *Money and Finance*, Volume Nos. 9-10, April-September 2002.

Rao, M.J.M. (1997): "Macro-Economics of Capital Account Convertibility," *Economic and Political Weekly*, December 20, 1997.

Reserve Bank of India (1997): *Report of The Committee on Capital Account Convertibility*, Reserve Bank of India., Mumbai.

Reserve Bank of India (2006): *Report of the Committee on Fuller Capital Account Convertibility*, www.rbi.org.in.

Rodrik, D. (1998): "Who Needs Capital Account Convertibilty?", www.ksg/Harvard/Rodrik/essay.PDF

Roy, M., R. Mishra and S. Mishra (2007): "A Review of Cross-Country Experience in Capital Account Liberalisation," *Reserve Bank of India Occasional Papers*, Vol. 27, Nos. 1 and 2, Summer and Monsoon, 2006.

Stiglitz, J.E. (2000): "Capital Market Liberalization, Economic Growth and Instability," *World Development*, Volume 28, No. 6.

3

Capital Account Liberalization and the Indian Economy

SMRITI MUKHERJEE

ABSTRACT

Debate about capital account liberalization arose in the wake of the debt crisis of 1980's when higher weightage was given to private capital flows and multilateral development lending as a means of solution of capital scarcity. Better allocation of capital required easing of capital control measures throughout the world and accordingly capital account liberalization was advocated.

The present paper discusses basically two issues namely how the accumulation of reserves after capital account liberalization is to be utilized and whether higher macroeconomic volatility following current convertibility as has happened in the case of certain other countries, is applicable to India.

The two episodes of surge in capital inflows during 1992-97—2002 to the present day did not result in any world wide crisis largely because roughly 1/3 of incoming flows was added to the reserves. Reserve accumulation meant foregoing of additional income on the part of the central bank since international reserves are put into 'reserve grade' assets earning very low rate of return. One solution can be to create access for domestic corporate sector to this fund so that they can compete in international markets. In that case change in the exchange rate will have substantial wealth effect and domestic interest rate will fluctuate more making way for macroeconomic instability.

To see whether a liberalized atmosphere in the country has resulted in greater income and consumption volatility we collected data over the forty year period 1960-61---1999-'00. Standard deviation of annual percentage growth rates were obtained for each of the four decades. Both income and consumption volatility were found to be following a declining trend after 1979-80. Magnitude of volatility for terms of trade, however was much higher than those of income and consumption but phenomenon of declining trend was present there also.

I. BACKGROUND

Resolution of the international debt crisis during the mid-eighties through debt buy-back, debt restructuring and debt rescheduling made it evident that a long lasting solution was needed to prevent the recurrence of the crisis. The financial obligation undertaken by the international agencies could not be repeated every now and then and irresponsible behaviour of lenders and borrowers in the commercial market had to be curbed also. In the mean time flow of official development assistance to the needy countries underwent substantial changes. Donor countries were no longer willing to direct their resources towards developing countries in general; instead they preferred to concentrate in favour of the least developed countries. Proportion of grants as against concessional loans was increased so that really poor countries need not bother about debt servicing. Loans started to be given for more specific purposes also like building better trade infrastructure. IMF itself was interested in giving technical assistance loan to increase the absorptive capacity of least developed countries regarding inflow of higher trade turnover. A time schedule was also insisted on so that efficiency in utilization gets its due importance.

The changed attitude of donor countries towards official development assistance meant drying up of one of the most important sources of foreign aid. The answer to the question lay in finding out alternative sources of financing and the idea of globalization already under way provided the ready answer to the problem.

II. WHY CAPITAL ACCOUNT LIBERALIZATION?

The most forceful argument in favour of capital account liberalization was probably given by Rodrik (1998) when he collected data for 100 countries over the period 1975-89 to show that per capita GDP growth depended negatively on the number of years a country has spent under liberalized capital flows. Contribution of capital mobility to growth was recognized and the finding added credence to the convergence hypothesis under which less developed countries were to experience higher rate of growth, thus closing the gap between rich and poor nations. Argument of democracy was also brought in to show that democratic countries like to have fewer controls on individual freedom including the freedom to manage one's finances. Why is it that developing countries tend to persist with capital controls? One major reason is associated with the urge to preserve scarce foreign exchange resources. In the absence of controls on capital movement more affluent among the domestic residents might be tempted to send their money abroad. To make sure that domestic saving is available for domestic investment it was inevitable. It resulted in misallocation of resources for the world economy as a whole but domestic injury was avoided.

The second important reason associated with capital controls was definitely the pegged exchange rate system advocated during Bretton Woods era. Unless restrictions were there on capital movements governments would find it very difficult to maintain the peg. To keep demand for imports within reasonable limits elaborate exchange control procedures were drawn up in the absence of which there would have been a run on international reserves. International liquidity was preserved to a great extent with the presence of capital controls.

Another reason, though a little bit far fetched seems to be the policy independence chosen by the domestic monetary authorities. If capital account is fully open domestic residents would have the freedom to own a part of their portfolio in the form of foreign currency assets. Now if it happens that monetary authorities are intent on following a restrictive monetary policy by resorting to open market purchase residents can avoid the impact by selling foreign currency assets and augmenting their liquidity. The same may happen in case reserve requirements are raised for the financial institutions. Central bank independence and effectiveness of monetary policy can be lost by having an early opening of capital account.

Lastly it can be pointed out that political philosophy being pursued just after the World War II was largely in favour of public sector led growth. Planned development put the onus of finding resources for development on the government and bilateral or multilateral sources of development aid were accorded prominence. To repose faith in private sources of capital required some strength on the part of an economy concerned. The infant industry psychology in the sphere of trade found its echo in protecting the domestic economy from outside influence as far as capital movements were concerned. Expectations of generating a substantial flow of funds from abroad were fragile while fear of unnecessary volatility was uppermost in the minds of policy makers.

III. THEORETICAL PERSPECTIVE

Balance of payments equilibrium issues, intimately associated with overall balance in the economy have been thoroughly discussed under internal and external balance phenomena. The relation between fiscal and current account balance can in fact, be traced to the concepts of internal and external balance. While internal balance refers to the maintenance of price stability and full employment, external balance refers to zero current account balance. If domestic absorption given by C+I+G should increase producing an excess demand situation external demand must come down to maintain price stability. This can be done by an appreciation of exchange rate so that aggregate absorption and exchange rate become inversely related. Again, if external demand should increase leading to a surplus in net export earnings internal demand must adjust to restore a zero current account balance. This is possible if aggregate absorption should increase producing a rise in income and higher demand for imports. External balance is preserved by maintaining a positive relation between domestic absorption and exchange rate.

The simple law of market tells us that equilibrium on both fronts will be achieved when the lines showing internal and external balance intersect. The point of intersection yields the equilibrium pair of domestic absorption and exchange rate. The crux of the matter is however not the establishment of equilibrium but the forces that lead to it. A combination of price stability and full employment on the one hand and zero current account balance on the other is made possible through a judicious mix of fiscal restraint and floating exchange rate. Exchange rate management has to play an active role in the pursuit of zero current account balance. Market determined exchange rate is vital for achieving current account equilibrium.

Let us explore this last point in somewhat more detail. Had it been a case of pegged exchange rate higher domestic income consequent upon a fiscal deficit would push up internal demand. To maintain aggregate demand at a given level net export earnings must come down which may be accomplished through an indirect route. Excess demand in domestic market would push up prices as a result of which real exchange rate would appreciate and external sector would end up with a deficit. A linkage between fiscal and monetary policy will also produce the same result since fiscal impulse is met by additional money creation. So rise in absorption would generate forces to contain external demand even under pegged exchange rate.

The adjustment problem in pegged exchange rate lies elsewhere. Lack of external equilibrium is a regular episode and any curtailments of internal absorption to maintain aggregate demand at a given level is extremely difficult to achieve. This is more so in the case of developing countries where cut in fiscal deficit might compromise with growth prospects of the economy. In the opposite case where a country has surplus in the current account the resulting increase in demand is not enough to produce additional import requirements that will eliminate the greater than zero current account balance.

The whole question of macroeconomic balance in an economy then settles down to the type of exchange rate management the economy is having market determined exchange rate only expected to ensure compatibility of internal and external balance. The condition of zero current balance emphasized in this approach might appear too restrictive for an economy to follow in the short-run and accordingly balancing problem has been extended to the entire balance of payments. Balance of payments is sum total of current and capital accounts so that a surplus in the current account, if accompanied by a deficit in the capital account, leaves us with a zero in the balance of payments which is identical with balance of payments equilibrium.

The two determining variables of external equilibrium in this case are income and interest rare as against absorption and exchange rate in the earlier approach. A rise in income produces current account deficit which can be offset by rise in interest rate leading to greater inflow of capital or surplus in the capital account. If one starts with a rise in interest rate first resulting in surplus in the capital account that would require a rise in income to push up demand for imports in the economy. The resulting deficit in current account would nullify the surplus in the capital account so that balance of payments equilibrium would continue to persist. Under the presence of capital mobility BoP equilibrium is given by an upward sloping straight line connecting income and the rate of interest.

In case an economy decides to open its capital account a close watch on domestic monetary and fiscal situation is essential to maintain balance of payments equilibrium. Capital account adjustment is conditional upon the ease with which domestic interest rate can move both up and down. Therefore, freeing of domestic interest rate from government control is a first order condition before opening up of capital account is attempted. Negative real rate before liberalization has to be converted into a positive one before free capital mobility is given a serious thought. A surge in capital inflow that has been experienced by many economies immediately after liberalization was largely made possible by favourable domestic interest rate differential.

The analysis we are talking about is silent on exchange rate arrangement, meaning thereby that capital account liberalization can be undertaken under both pegged and floating rate (managed or full) schemes. Under pegged rate there is one danger that hedging may not be given due attention because everybody expects the current exchange rate to prevail in future also. Unless hedging to cover currency risk is undertaken future market cannot develop in foreign exchange and ability of spot rate to move according to market expectations gets greatly impaired. Precautionary holding of foreign currency generally does not take place under pegged rate. To that extent it might encourage too much spending of foreign currency. Reckless spending might precipitate a financial crisis under liberalization with pegged rate.

A problem common with both pegged and floating exchange rates is the sudden escalation in asset prices and stock market valuations. Portfolio funds find their way into the local stock market and an asset market bubble like situation might develop. Bubbles have the probability of bursting if substantial reverse flows should occur. An appropriate mix of direct and portfolio funds can prevent this sort of situation. An unduly large inflow of portfolio capital accompanied by lack of real sector development might result in temporary loss of confidence in the economy and prompt withdrawal of capital. Composition of capital inflow can tell a lot about possibility of an emerging crisis.

IV. CURRENT INTERNATIONAL SCENARIO ABOUT CAPITAL ACCOUNT LIBERALIZATION

Globalization has imparted tremendous boost to both trade and financial sector integration. The number of countries with convertibility in current account (many of whom have capital account convertibility also) has gone up from 62 in 1990 to 164 in 2004. The international consensus seems to hover around three points:

(I) an exchange rate system that is more responsive to market forces,

(II) gradual opening of the capital account, and
(III) a monetary policy that favours price stability.

Once a country liberalizes the current account it is expected that steps would be taken to open the capital account within a reasonable period of time. The constraints to be fulfilled are a low inflation rate, low fiscal deficit, a well-regulated financial system and an adequate reserve level to act as a buffer against capital flight.

Already two episodes of heavy influx of private capital have been noticed, one lasted between 1992-97 and the second one started in 2002 and continues till date. The general consequences of this upsurge have been a rise in investment-GDP ratio, considerable amount of appreciation in exchange rate and a substantial reserve accumulation. Occasional encounter with financial crisis has been there but their impact has been mostly localized.

For developing countries rise in investment-GDP ratio signifies a breakthrough in domestic investment scenario. Non-insurable risk is being shared by international community and that is a healthy sign. Appreciation of exchange rate is but expected and this is necessary to produce a current account deficit that will make up for capital account surplus. In fact, some writers in the early eighties have hinted upon the idea of a substantial depreciation in national currency for the countries intending to have a liberalization of capital account. A devaluation of say, 25 per cent, would leave considerable scope for future exchange rate appreciation. Sudden jump in current account surplus will gradually be eroded by the surging capital inflows. The third point of accumulation of official reserves requires some detailed scrutiny.

Most of the developing countries going in for liberalization of capital account has diverted about 1/3 of capital for reserves build-up. This has prevented excessive rise in aggregate demand leading to higher rate of inflation. Viewed from another angle piling up of reserves has a definite cost associated with it. Normally central bank buys up whole or a major part of incoming flows in exchange of national currency or government securities. Expansion of monetary base has the potential of creating or adding to the inflationary potential in the economy. And the domestic agents having access to larger liquidity will give a push to the aggregate demand curve. With a view to preventing expansion in money supply central bank periodically engages in open market sale of government securities which is better known as sterilization operation. Such sales by themselves can impart a push to interest rate by depressing asset prices. That in turn might lead to further inflow of private funds from abroad.

Holding of sizeable quantity of reserves is not a paying proposition for the central bank either. Foreign exchange is never held in liquid form; it is invested in reserve grade assets. The interest rate earned on such foreign currency assets is nowhere near the interest earned on domestic securities so that holding of large amount of reserves indicates a revenue loss for the central government. Had it been made available to domestic portfolio holders they might make their presence felt in the international market. Private portfolio holders have a larger horizon and release of funds to them might result in shifting of the risk on the part of the central bank.

Utilizing piled up reserves in this fashion absolves central bank of the responsibility for foregoing extra income no doubt, but it is fraught with another type of problem. Exposure to foreign financial markets might increase the risk taking probability in the face of domestic shocks by a particular class having access to international capital. This is likely to have impact on domestic income as well as consumption volatility through the wealth effect. A rise in the exchange rate would lead to an increase in the domestic currency value of foreign assets and that would augment the value of financial wealth. It may lead to asset substitution whereby foreign assets would he replaced by money or domestic bonds or both. Higher demand for money with supply remaining constant would push up domestic interest rates. Similarly higher demand for domestic assets would imply a fall in the asset market interest rate. In both cases changes in the interest rate are brought about by forces outside the domestic monetary system.

A third possibility of impact on the domestic market arises from the fact that rise in wealth may promote rise in consumption expenditure. Being assured of access to international markets the well-off group might indulge in excessive consumption. This phenomenon will be restricted to a particular section whereas the others with no access to international market will suffer due to a rise in commodity prices. They will have poor insurance against this commodity price rise shock. The net impact will be increased volatility of consumption expenditure. Income volatility will also increase because of the fact that one group of people is having more exposure due to financial integration and it is this group which precisely acts channels of transmission as long as central bank is able to prevent transfer of reserves to other lucrative income earning avenues the domestic economy is protected against this additional source of volatility. Whether higher income and consumption volatility lead to higher growth happens to be the ultimate deciding factor. If a higher growth rate emerges through higher consumption expenditure volatility, central bank can safely think of sharing excessive reserve holding risk with domestic portfolio holders.

V. EFFORTS TOWARDS INTEGRATION AND MACROECONOMIC VOLATILITY IN INDIA

Discussions about financial sector integration are invariably associated with questions about volatility. Greater financial flows often lead to disruption in economic life resulting in crisis. Appearance of such crisis is preceded by volatility of serious proportions in important variables like income, consumption, asset prices and sometimes in terms of trade also. The magnitude of volatility happens to be higher in the case of developing as against developed countries which has been well documented by several people. What is more interesting is that consumption volatility happens to be higher in relation to income volatility giving credence to the view that financial integration causes higher instability in the case of consumption. The reasons are that more and more people gain access to the capital market as a result of which temporary increases in consumption are more likely. Higher economic endowment finds current consumption temporarily deviating from its long-run stable relationship with income.

People attempting an empirical testing of increased macroeconomic volatility or higher consumption volatility mostly base their analysis on post integration data. In the Indian case trade integration has been much more compared to that in the financial sector but still then some exercise could be attempted to shed light on volatility debate. Accordingly we decided to test volatility in regard to per capita GDP (both at current and constant prices), per capita GNP (both at current and constant prices), per capita private final consumption expenditure (both at current and constant prices). GNP was included to make the calculations more broad based since factor income from abroad will also be included. Volatility was measured by standard deviation of annual percentage growth rates of income and consumption over the period 1960-61 to 1999-2000. The whole period was divided into four decades and standard deviations were obtained for each decade. No overall estimate for the entire forty year period was attempted. The results are given below.

TABLE I

Volatility of Growth Rates of Income, Consumption and Terms of Trade

Variables	*Decades*			
	1960-69	*1970-1979*	*1980-89*	*1990-*
GDP per capita (current price)	4.6026	5.3189	3.0844	2.20
GDP per capita (1993-94P)	3.4796	3.9698	2.1445	1.75
GNP per capita (current price)	4.8127	5.4813	3.3350	1.99
GNP per capita (1993-94P)	3.7617	4.2635	1.2486	1.98
PFCE per capita (current P)	6.2561	11.2438	5.4081	2.43
PFCE per capita (1993-94P)	1.9016	3.0655	2.2390	2.24
Net TOT (1978-79=100)		14.7680	12.1584	9.70

Note: Years indicate fiscal periods like 1980-81—1989-90, 1990-91---1999-2000, etc.

The results show that there is no evidence in support of higher income and consumption volatility following attempts towards integration. Rather all volatility figures stage a consistent decline during the last two decades, i.e. 1980-81-1989-90 and 1990-91—1999-2000. In some developed countries GNP shows wider volatility compared to GDP figures but that is not found to be true in the case of the Indian economy. The Table reveals just one important information that volatility of selected variables we have calculated reached a peak during the decade 1970-71—1979-80. Subsequently it started declining and liberalization attempts did not reverse the trend.

Net terms of trade fluctuation was seen to be the highest amongst the three variables we have selected for studying. But it also shared the same feature of the highest volatility during the seventies and subsequent smoothing out. If degree of specialization and hence commodity concentration is very high, trade integration might result in greater instability. The whole brunt of adjustment will have to be shared by a handful of commodities whereas lesser trade dependence acts as a cushion for transmitting disturbances. In the case of the economies where trade integration acted as the precursor, capital account liberalization increased terms of trade volatility was looked upon as an adverse signal. Unless terms of trade volatility is held under check, risk might be more for financial integration. For one thing upsurge in capital inflow would disturb the exchange rate and terms of volatility would further aggravate it. Fortunately no perceptible higher volatility in terms of trade was noticed in the case of the Indian economy.

VI. CONCLUSION

Since India has liberalized her current account the general expectation both within and outside the country about the capital account liberalization has gone up. That the matter is under active consideration of the Reserve Bank of India is evident from the appointment of a special committee in this regard. The central question facing any country contemplating capital account liberalization is the possible cost and benefit associated with such a step. The present paper as can be seen tries to shed some light on the cost aspect of financial liberalization by focusing on macroeconomic volatility. Economic theory prediction about greater volatility following trade or capital account liberalization is far from conclusive. Thus some authors have found evidence that income volatility increases after liberalization but consumption volatility declines. Now decrease in consumption volatility probably works through wealth effect. Changes in the interest rate or exchange rate marks changes in asset valuation and that may be an additional source of financing consumption expenditure. Increased current account balances contribute to higher income partially but greater amount of it may be credited to foreign asset purchases. Similarly when there is a decrease in income, consumption may decline much less than that predicted by the marginal propensity to consume owing to the cushion provided by asset holding. Thus smoothing of consumption over cycles can be explained with the help of wealth effect after loosening of capital account restrictions.

Those who cite greater volatility after capital market integration must be concentrating on external shocks and their transmission. Transmission of monetary and fiscal policy shocks become easier due to higher interdependence brought about by financial integration. Even terms of trade shocks may be pronounced once protection offered by tariffs is removed. Removal of distortions and prevalence of world market prices would transmit shocks in a direct manner. Severe terms of trade shocks may spell disaster for balance of payments and that can precipitate domestic macroeconomic crisis. This kind of result is valid for the economies having a high trade share in GDP. In the case of the Indian economy still now the passage linking the domestic economy with the rest of the world is not sufficiently broad based.

The present paper was not written with a view to ascertaining whether time is ripe for capital account convertibility in India. We have examined the theoretical background and how the economy is progressing under current account convertibility. Increased volatility in either income or consumption serves as a danger signal for complete opening up of capital account. The opportunity cost of opening up then tends to be rather high. Further research is necessary to find out if net benefits from capital account liberalization is likely to be greater than zero.

References

Arumugam, S. (2006): 'Neoclassical Finance and the Fully Convertible Rupee,' *EPW*, Vol. XLI, No. 4, Nov. 18-24, pp. 4807-14.

Bakker, A. and B. Chapple (2002): Advanced Country Experiences with Capital Account Liberalization', *IMF Occasional Paper*, No. 214.

Calvo, G.A. (2003): 'Explaining--Sudden Stop, Growth Collapse and BOP Crisis; *IMF Staff Papers*, Vol. 50, pp. 1-20.

Eichengreen, B. (2001): 'Capital Account Liberalization: What do Cross Country Studies Tell Us?', *The World Bank Economic Review*, Vol. 15, No. 3, pp. 341-66.

Economic and Political Weekly, XLI 19, 2006, a few articles.

Ghosh, A., (2002): Timothy Lane and others, 'IMF Supported Programs in Capital Account Crisis', *IMF Occasional Paper* 210.

lshii, S. and K. Habermeier (2002): 'Capital Account Liberalization and Financial Sector Stability', *IMF Occasional Paper* 211.

Kletzer, K. and Mark M. Spiegel (2004): 'Sterilization Costs and Exchange Rate Targetting', *Journal of International Money and Finance*, 23(6), pp. 897-915.

Kose M.A.., E. Prasad and M.E.T. Terrons (2005): Financial Integration and Macroeconomic Volatility, *IMF Staff Papers*, Vol. 50, pp. 119-42.

Levchenko, A. (2005): 'A Financial Liberalization and Consumption Volatility in Developing Countries', *IMF Staff Papers*, Vol. 52, No. 2, pp. 237-59.

Minlane, J., 'A New Set of Measures on Capital Account Restrictions', *IMF Staff Papers*, Vol. 52, No. 2, pp. 276-308.

Quirk, P.J. and O. Evans (1995): 'Capital Account Convertibility', *IMF Occasional Paper* 131.

Reserve Bank of India (1997): *Report of the Committee on Capital Account Convertibility*.

World Bank (2006): *Global Development Finance*.

4

Capital Account Convertibility in India: Some Theoretical Issues and Policy Perscriptions

Asim K. Karmakar

Abstrct

One of the hotly debated issues in the arena of Indian economics in recent years is tile full capital account convertibility (CA C) that arises in the context when by the mid-1990s, the Indian economy improved its BoP and forex reserve position. Several countries in Asia and Latin America have adopted full convertibility of their currencies in pursuing the policy of liberalization and reform. Whether a time is right for India to move towards full convertibility is now a moot question, though the IMF and the several committees set up in India is in high favour to ensure a smooth transition towards fuller CAC enamoured with vibrant fiscal consolidation, a strong banking system, sustainable current account deficit and appropriate maintenance of external debt and forex reserves. And India meanwhile has already gone for an adventure in its way towards full CAC. The present paper gives an account of the basic theoretical issues that have arisen in international discussions on CAC and India's standpoint on this issue in particular. An attempt has also been made here to deal essentially with the arguments for and against international capital mobility, with an assessment of how the Indian economy has been moving from exchange control to the gradual, step by step approach towards CAC.

I. INTRODUCTION

One of the most hotly debated issues that crops up in the context of the currency and banking crisis experienced by several countries of East Asia that erupted from July 1997, traveling from Thailand to Indonesia, Malaysia and South Korea by December 1997 as well as those seen in Russia in 1998 and Brazil and Euro-Zones most recently is that of capital account convertibility (CAC) of the balance of payments (BoP) of developing countries. Among developed countries, the US was the first one that went in for CAC in 1974. Between 1979 till 1991, most of the European countries, Japan, Australia and New Zealand also adopted full capital account liberalization although patterns as well as time taken varied between countries. The IMF nowadays proposes that all its member-countries should make their currencies freely convertible for all current as well as capital account transactions.

The paper presents a brief sketch of the basic theoretical issues that have arisen in international discussions on CAC and India's standpoint in this issue in particular.

With the displacement of pegged exchange rates by a regime of floating rates in the 1970s, a new orthodoxy begins to campaign that free capital mobility is of utmost importance for maximizing global benefits from international trade and investments. The floating market determined exchange rate determined by the forces of demand and supply and the lifting of capital controls were considered essential steps in the establishment of an efficient international financial system. The argument was that full convertibility on capital account will bring about equilibrium in the external sector of developing countries by bringing in capital flow to finance whatever current account gap that may result in if only interest rate is put to a high level. This argument is in line with the Mundell-Fleming Open Economy Model which extends the Keynesian Fix-Price Model for well developed domestic financial markets.

The new orthodoxy is also vociferous on capital mobility, but the peculiar thing is that there has not grown any consensus on the true exchange rate regime. However, the IMF defines CAC as the 'freedom from exchange controls on capital transactions in the BoP' within either a fixed or a flexible exchange rate regime. India has accepted the goal of capital account convertibility as part of the ongoing liberalization process. The Tarapore Committee, appointed by the RBI has looked into the issues and prospects of undertaking CAC in India. The Committee set up in February 1997 has given a pragmatic working definition of CAC as "the freedom to convert local financial assets to foreign financial assets and *vice versa* at market determined exchange rate, without needing any permission from the government. It is associated with changes of ownership in foreign/domestic financial assets and liabilities and embodies the creation and liquidation of claims on, or by, the rest of the world. CAC can be, and is, coexistent with restrictions other than on external payments. It also does not preclude the imposition of monetary/fiscal measures relating to foreign exchange transactions which are of a prudential nature." In other words, CAC implies complete mobility of free and unregulated capital funds across countries.The report of the committee on CAC, submitted at end-May 1997, had a road map for moving towards CAC by 1999-2000. The Tarapore Committee recommended in May 1997 (RBI, 1997) that CAC should be conditional on a set of stringent requirements, including fiscal consolidation, low inflation, strict supervision and regulation of financial institutions, and financial restructuring, besides keeping watch on BoP and the quantum of foreign exchange reserves. The absence of a fully open capital account places limits on large-scale capital transfers without short period of time. To examine the issue of CAC afresh, the RBI on 20 March, 2006, appointed the second Tarapore Committee (Tarapore II). Tarapore II observed that there was progress towards CAC, '... on an *ad hoc* basis and the liberalized framework continues to be a prisoner of the erstwhile strict control system.' The Committee recommended measures such as reduction of the gross borrowing requirement of the government, adopting the public sector borrowing requirement (PSBR) as a clear indicator of the public sector deficit, setting up of an Office of Public Debt outside the RBI and a clear setting of monetary policy objectives jointly by the government and RBI, for fuller CAC. The Committee recommended a gradual approach towards fuller CAC consisting of thee phases, with 2006-07 being the first phase, 2007-09 the second phase, 2010-12 be the third and the final phase. The substantive recommendations of Tarapore II included raising the annual ceiling on external commercial borrowing (ECB), relaxing restrictions on rupee-denominated and on long-maturity ECBs, easing up on FII investment in debt securities, and liberalizing outward investment by both individuals and corporates. On December 20, 2006, RBI completed the first phase of fuller CAC and allowed the Indian residents to remit USD 50,000 for any current and capital account transactions or a combination of both. Indian Investors are now free to buy property or share or any other assets abroad without any prior approval of the regulator, RBI. Now Indians are able to invest in any listed foreign entity. Additionally, this liberalization will offer individual to open, maintain and hold foreign currency accounts with a bank outside India without prior approval of the RBI. The PM committee and the Rajan Committee also have unanimously recommended a move towards fuller CAC. The PM Committee has observed that India had a de facto open capital account for the real economy, but not for financial services. Lack of capital account convertibility has reduced competition in the Indian financial sector and denied the country to have competition-induced efficiency gains. In its report, the PM Committee argued for introduction of full CAC, an inflation-targeted monetary policy, a move from the rule-based and fragmented to a principles-based and unified financial sector regularity texture. Some experts go even far ahead to say that the benefits from CAC for the financial sector in India will be analogous to the benefits that accrued to the real sector from the policy of opening up in the early 1990s.

In this paper an attempt has also been made to deal essentially with the arguments for and against international capital mobility, with a brief sketch of the simple macroeconomic of BoP transactions, because an understanding of the link between the current and capital account is crucial in understanding the issues involved in the discussion on CAC.

II. CONCEPTUAL ISSUES

As we all know that gross national product (GNP) may be considered from either the product side (demand) or the factor payments side (supply). On the product side, we have

$$Y=C+I+G+X-M \quad \text{...(i)}$$

where Y is GNP, C is consumption, I is investment, G is government purchases, X is exports, and M is imports.

On the factor payments side, we have

$$Y=C+Sp+T \quad \text{....(ii)}$$

where C is again consumption, Sp is private saving, and T is tax revenue.

We may subtract equation (ii) from equation (i) to obtain

$$0=(I-Sp) + [G-T] + [X-M]$$

Rearranging, we may identify the resource gap as:

$$M-X=(I-Sp) + (G-T)$$

Thus, the excess of imports over exports must equal the excess of investment over private saving plus the excess of government purchases over tax revenue. Considering that the government's fiscal balance is tax revenue minus government spending or T-G and that this balance may be thought of as government's saving (Sg), we now rewrite the resource gap as:

$$M-X=I-Sp-(T-G)=I-Sp-Sg=I-(Sp+Sg)=I-S$$

where S is the total of all saving, government plus private. Thus, the need for the external resources, and therefore the trade gap, equals the excess of domestic investment over total domestic savings. Similarly, (X-M) is the surplus in the trade account. If we add to it invisible trade and unrequited transfer payments, we have the current account of BoP. If we assume for simplicity, that such receipts are zero, then the current account surplus has to be matched by excess of saving over investment and the budget surplus. In this perspective, a deficit in the current account implies insufficient saving relative to investment and government spending.

Since the overall BoP always balances, we now have to look towards the BoP in the capital account. The capital account records all international transactions that involve a resident of a country changing either his or her assets with, or liabilities to, a resident of another country and consists of short-term and long-term private official flows towards, portfolio and direct investment, and changes in official resources. In fact, capital account transactions can involve changes in the composition of the national capital of the country. In what follows, a deficit in the current account will always imply a surplus in the capital account and vice versa that also means inflow of foreign funds has to supplement domestic savings.

And the net inflow of foreign funds through the capital account meets the excess requirements of investible funds over domestic savings in the economy. In fact, the following relationships hold between the current and the capital accounts, from two sides:

Current account deficit = capital account surplus + drawing down of reserves

Or

Surplus in the current account = (X-M) = S-I+T-G=Change in Net foreign assets.

This means that if a country has a deficit on its current account, the country has spent more abroad that it has earned during the specified period. This can be settled by international borrowing, or by seeking capital flows in the form of direct or portfolio investment or by depleting reserve accumulations of foreign currency that have built up over the years. Now any changes in the capital account of BoP, brought about by autonomous capital 'flows' get reflected through changes either in the current account position or the reserve position.

The decision to allow the free flow of direct and financial foreign capital across national boundaries can thus have serious implications for the national sovereignty of a country.

A substantial inflow of capital sometimes distort the medium and long-term fundamental of an economy as it happened in case of Mexico in 1995, East Asia in mid-1997, and Euro-Zones during 1999-2000. Even if economic fundamentals remain strong, a country may be highly vulnerable to speculative attacks with high current account deficits.

However, large capital inflows or outflows affect the domestic economy in a variety of ways. For example, within a flexible exchange rate regime, excessive inflows of capital results in an appreciation of the domestic currency and thereby affect the competitiveness of the host country in the international goods market, on the one hand, and widens the trade deficits by increasing imports, on the other. This results in the possibility of increasing current account deficits that can become unsustainable. The central bank's intervention to avoid these effects causes problems and affects the independent monetary operation, while on the other way, capital outflows in a flexible exchange rate regime tend to depreciate the domestic currency and can cause inflationary pressures and can induce capital flight.

So the exact choices for the appropriate exchange rate determination along with whether and how to control capital flows have become crucial. Second, the maintenance of high interest rate concerning incoming of foreign portfolio flows can adversely affect productive investment directly and it also makes public debt servicing more expensive. Thus opening up of global portfolio flows may result in stagnation of the country since portfolio investment comes to a country when the BoP position of a country is good. Hence the debate whether a country should liberalize capital account transactions, or not and, if they do so, how this should be done.

III. OVER THE CAC DEBATE HOVERING AROUND INDIA

The essence of CAC is a liberalization of outflows for residence. Convertibility for non-residence on the capital account in India has all along been available. In fact, there is full convertibility for portfolio flows through foreign institutional investors (FIIs) as far as equity markets are concerned. Currently, there is virtually full CAC for Indian corporates. However, discussion on liberalization of the capital account on the BOP essentially revolve around whether or not to restrict the free movement of capital across the national boundaries and, if a free flow is deemed a desirable objective, how and why it should be introduced in the context of an overall liberalization programme in India.

The basic issue of capital account liberalization has been to integrate the domestic capital market with the free working of the international capital market so that various policy- induced distortions stemming from multitude of controls in the domestic capital market are eliminated and the law of arbitrage (which takes into account of the riskless purchase of a product in one market for immediate resale in a second market in order to profit from price differences between the markets) prevails in the capital account transactions. This again calls for systematic dismantling of controls and elimination of informational asymmetries such that arbitrage conditions prevail and the capital market functions smoothly. But the encouragement of the arbitrage operation for which banks, non-bank financial institutions and individuals would prefer to borrow global capital cheap and resell it in a second market immediately in order to profit, would increase not only the external debt burden of the country but also encourage the functioning of the black economy and financial instability because of the heavy investment in physical and financial assets. Moreover, full CAC often provides wrong signals to the international investors about the host country's economic fundamentals. Since the international investors are mainly concerned about their profit maximisation rather than productive investment, they mobilize their funds for higher returns which may result in moral hazard and adverse selection problems and thereby destabilize the financial system and cause great loss to the host countries. Above all, CAC puts new pressures on the overall macroeconomic management of the economy in that poor macroeconomic policies will invariably generate large outflows of funds, and price volatility.

One can easily point out that the present Indian situation is not ripen enough to go into for full convertibility on capital accounts on the account that full convertibility involves freeing capital markets. Unless and until the rupee is freely floated, this would complicate the task of the exchange rate management. With large capital flows there can be an unsustainable appreciation of the rupee and when the market assessment is that appreciation is unsustainable, there can be sudden capital outflows and an uncontrollable spiral of depreciation of currency.

The globalization of capital has had its discontents. In the aftermath of Asian crisis, many academics and policy-makers blamed volatile, speculative capital flows for the virulence of this financial crisis and their contagion effects. For example, the introduction of CAC in the case of South Korea was the chief culprit for the virulence of the crisis. The collapse of the currency in that country was the resultant of so many factors like accumulation of short-term foreign loans, the gradual loss of confidence of foreign managers who actually flocked together to East and South Asia on the look out for higher returns and the contagion effect of crises in neighbouring countries. This crisis led to a breakdown of international finance and resulted in costly adjustment for those economies. Besides, hasty capital account liberalization will lead to speculative attack on the exchange rate as it happened in other countries. Thirdly, financial openness index for the Indian economy is still very low in comparison to the other countries. Fourthly, the inadequate liberalization in the domestic financial and banking sector may cause to greater volatility. Fifthly, full capital account convertibility will put a pressure on the trade balance of the economy, as it is told earlier. Another thing may happen, following an increase in the interest rate structure in the developed countries with CAC as a step, like sudden withdrawal of foreign funds invested through the foreign financial institutions. This happens in India and now it is apprehended that the resources mobilized through the Mutual Funds have been channelled into the share market without adequate preparation resulting in an artificial upward trend in the share prices. As a consequence, there has been a crash as well as instability in the share market. This problem may have the implications of distant thunder, and it may cause adverse effect on the employment situation. Finally, India has had the past memories of an acute shortage of foreign exchange. Capital outflows by overseas deposits by Indian investors will fetch a lower return as well as a currency risk for the Indian investors. One must draw lessons from the recent history of Latin America where the outflow of capital pushed a number of countries into debt trap and towards "casino capitalism." Nay, a review of the international experience with CAC shows that liberalization of the capital account induces large capital inflows which can cause real appreciation in the exchange rate and erode the effectiveness of the domestic monetary policy. It is often been argued nowadays that the developed countries always give pressure on developing countries to adopt CAC. This argument can be very simply understood in terms of the imperatives of sustaining the US deficit. The leading countries of the world have a large and mounting external deficit which they finance by issuing debt in their own countries, while absorbing savings and capital from the rest of the world. The open financial market of the developing countries has always provided a safety valve for the US dollar by sustaining the growing deficits. Capital flight from these developing countries allows the US to maintain its deficits.

Moreover, an open capital account imposes tremendous pressures on the financial system and brings weaknesses in the financial system into sharper focus. Thus the critics argue that in the absence of complementary macro-economic policies, full scale liberalization of capital account will pose much more danger to the Indian economy as is not comprehended by the Tarapore Committee (*Chatterjee*, 1998). Even in recent times, the central government's keen attitude to take the economic reforms on the path of fuller CAC as is indicated by the appointment of the Raghuram Rajan Committee has been harshly criticised by Amiya Kumar Bagchi (2009) when he says, "the interim report (of the Committee) is one of the most egregious exercises in rich men's ideology that I have come across." Despite the international experience of full convertibility of a developing country currency being regularly attended by a currency crisis and banking crisis and despite the warnings of practically all leading economists of home and abroad about the dangers of the move, the government of (our country) has moved far in that direction, allowing Indian corporate firms to borrow abroad and invest abroad (*Bagchi*, 2009).

160 leading economists had already issued a statement against CAC. Implementing CAC will imbalance our forex reserves. Lawrence Summers, Clinton's Treasury Secretary argues," India's 15 per cent forex reserves are in excess. In such a case if CAC is implemented, it will hike this figure more and the value of our domestic currency will appreciate, in turn, it will badly effect out export trade because the depreciated value of the foreign currency will reduce out corporate earnings." If our policy-designers now think that by implementing CAC in India will bring more capital flows, think of China. Even China does not have any modal of CAC, it has restricted capital inflows, still it has more capital inflows than India.

Now a pertinent question is whether there are any benefits from CAC. Advocates in its favour articulate that there would be some distinct advantages in the following manners:

- With CAC, the Indian resident will be able to use the world capital market for risk diversification and maximize the return on their resources. For example, in a situation for bad year in India, when financial assets generate a poor return, foreign assets owned by Indians would continue to generate good returns.

- By allowing residents to diversify their portfolio into foreign assets, such convertibility can reduce the variability of their income and wealth from domestic shocks and diffuse the risk of asset-price bubble.
- Convertibility would enable aggregate saving and investment to be optimised.
- Rates of return on debt and equity in India are high by world standard. With CAC, foreign money will come into India to reduce these rates of return. That is to say, the cost of capital faced by the companies of India in equity and debt financing would come down as there will be large inflow of capital in the country. At a lower cost of capital, more investment projects would be viable, which will generate a faster pace of investment and growth in the economy.
- It has been noted that over a period of time capital account controls and restrictions tend to turn progressively ineffective, costly and even distortive. Hence the need for capital account convertibility.
- There will be gains from free inflow and outflow of capital. Indian residents, Indian banks, Indian mutual funds, Indian corporates (if the corporates find it remunerative with joint ventures), would be able to enhance their earnings, by investing a part of their money and resources.
- There will be an availability of a large dose of capital at international prices to supplement domestic resources and if there is large capital inflows CAC would relieve pressure on the exchange rate, the monetary aggregates and thereby enhance the effectiveness of domestic policy.
- The spread of financial intermediaries will come down as result of increased competition and as such the system would be more efficient
- Tax evasion and capital flight will reduce since tax levels would come down to international level.

- The cost of government borrowing will come down as the rate of interest would be low and ultimately fiscal deficit will reduce.
- Capital outflows will propel Indian authorities to initiate corrective macroeconomic policies, for which Indian interest rates and stock prices would be highly attractive and Indian holding foreign financial assets abroad would find it attractive to invest in India.

In this perspective, the advocates also argue that India just cannot remain isolated in an increasingly integrating world. If India does not plan for an orderly integration with the world economy, the world would integrate with it in a manner in which India would have no control over events. Thus the question is whether or not we should move to CAC but whether we want an orderly or a disorderly transition to CAC of the Indian rupee (*Tarapore*, 2003).

IV. INDIA'S MOVE FROM EXCHANGE CONTROL TO CONVERTIBILITY

Since 1950, licensing of imports, imposition of high duties and stringent foreign exchange controls were part of the package of policy measures in India. This import substituting self-reliance strategy of 1950-80 with whom the Raj Krishna-mentioned Hindu annual rate of growth of 3.5% was intimately connected during the same period, has not eventually delivered significantly improved quality of life to the vast majority of population.

In the early and mid-1980s, policy changes were initiated. Relaxation of import controls, enhanced export initiatives and reduced controls on selected industries marked the beginnings of mild or modest doses of economic liberalization. The exchange rate policy, too, for the first time, was flexibly administered, allowing steady depreciation of the real exchange rate through continuously downward adjustment in the nominal exchange rate.

During the 1990s and beyond, the exchange rate regime has undergone significant changes. From a managed floating system under which the exchange rate was officially determined, the regime has passed through several phases to reach a market based system. Since March 1993, the rupee has been convertible on trade account, and the exchange rate of the rupee has been determined on the basis of underlying demand and supply conditions in the inter-bank market. Current account transactions like trade, tourism, travel, education abroad and in India, and remittances into and out of India for purchasing health-care products, etc. have been freed of exchange control regulations and controls over several transactions on capital account have been eased. While the central bank of the country intervenes in the foreign exchange market, it does so primarily to prevent volatility and instability.

The rupee has been convertible on current account on the logic that it would minimize the need for enforcement. In a country where enforcement is weak, exchange control simply encourages black market (hawala) transactions and corruption among enforcement officials. Therefore, it is imprudent to have exchange controls which encourage currency smuggling and black money and an increase in Bhagwatian 'DUP' activities. Secondly, attracting foreign investments is impossible if there are far too many controls, licenses and permits. Importantly, if remittances of profits and interest receipts in the case of bank deposits and dividends/earnings from portfolio investments are subject to exchange controls, the regime will act as a disincentive for foreign investors in the present day scenario where there are other countries which are keen to offer better facilities and fewer restrictions. Thirdly, the trade and exchange control regime in India did not generate a healthy export growth until the late 1970s and 1980s. Moreover, both per capita export and the export to GNP percentage were both relatively low in India in comparison with China, Indonesia, South Korea, Malaysia and Thailand. Controls on exchange transactions imply an overvalued exchange rate. The overvalued exchange rate may dissuade exporters to reap the benefits of export earnings into the country and dampen domestic savings. A similar reasoning applies to inward remittances. The country lost billions of dollars through the so-called processes of under- invoicing of exports and over-invoicing of imports. Lastly, a market-based exchange rate and a well-functioning exchange market provide an appropriate benchmark prices for goods and services as well as promote domestic economic efficiency, especially when currency convertibility is accompanied by trade liberalization.

The above arguments pointed to the need for convertibility on current account. However, export growth, inward remittances, FDI and allocative efficiency will not depend on currency convertibility alone; in most cases, other complementary measures suited to the context like trade liberalization in general, expanding outlets for foreign currency conversion and simplification of procedures for industrial investment are also important.

Current account convertibility has been successfully implemented in India since 1991. Now India is walking towards the road to capital account convertibility. In view of the rapid changes that have taken place over the last few years and the growing integration of the Indian economy with the world economy with the external sector now accounting for almost 40 per cent of GDP, for which the economy cannot be fully immune to international developments, the RBI has recently set up a committee comprising eminent policy-makers, financial-sector experts and numbers of the academia to suggest a roadmap for fuller CAC (Tarapore II). The committee is required to, in this context, examine the implications of fuller CAC on monetary and exchange rate management, financial markets and the financial system.

We address here the question whether time is ripe for capital account convertibility in India.

To pave the way for the success of Indian CAC, the First and the Second Tarapore Committee provide a certain set of preconditions, sequencing and timing of measures. For example India must maintain a mandated rate of inflation on an average 3-5 per cent for the three-year period 1997-98 to 1999-2000, must reduce its gross fiscal deficit as a percentage of GDP from 4.5 in 1997-98 to 4% in 1998-99 and further to 3.5% in 1999-2000, maintain its current account deficit at 1.6%

of GDP, but the present statistics for India goes the other way round. For example, average inflation rate at India is nearly 5% during 2001-02 to 2005-06, which goes against the Tarapore target rate. It is also difficult task before the Government to achieve Tarapore target of fiscal deficit to the tune of 3.5% of GDP, while the actual average fiscal deficit during 2000-01 to 2005-06 is found to be 5% of GDP. The CAC Committee has also recommended that the ratio of short-term debt plus portfolio stock as a percentage of foreign exchange reserve should not exceed 60%. Recent RBI Annual Report has indicated that this ratio is around 75%.Even the Committee recommended reduction of non-performing assets of Scheduled Commercial Banks as a percentage to total advances by 5% during 1997-98 to 1999-2000 has not been met over the years. So we may articulate that India should embark on full CAC from a position of a strength—a satisfactory real rate of growth, a relatively low inflation and a high level of forex reserves, a low current account deficit in BOP and a falling debt service ratio.

V. CONCLUSIONS

In what follows is that CAC has been no doubt a hotly debated topic nowadays in India and the subject matter of three officially-sponsored Reports: Tarapore II Reports, Mistry Reports(or the PM Committee Reports) and Rajan Reports. One can reasonably argue in this connection that all of these reports need to be reviewed, rethought and revisited in the light of the recent global economic and financial crisis which was triggered by the US sub-prime mortgage market in early 2007 and then spread all over the world and abated not yet because a semi-open country like India is more and more integrating with the global capital market and the large magnitude of its impact is vigorously felt on its economy.

CAC in India requires several prerequisites in terms of strong macroeconomic policy framework and soundness and efficiency of financial systems and markets in the light of macro-prudential regulations instead of the existing system of purely microeconomic regulation. Even the policy-makers of

India may alter in any way the current macroeconomic policy toward CAC, if necessary for India's growth from a development perspective. Jagdish Bhagwati's interesting comment on the risks of CAC in this context becomes more relevant when he says, "cease and desist from moving rapidly to full convertibility until you have gained political stability, economic prosperity and substantial macroeconomic expertise—and not just transparency and better banking supervision." However, the management of the external sector must be accompanied here by a flexible exchange rate, sustainable current account deficit, preference to non-debt creating resource flows, limits on the quantum, use and cost of external debt, and a highly restrictive approach to short-term debt along with encompassing a spectrum of other policy choices, which include the appropriate level of reserves, monetary policy objectives related to liquidity management and interest rates and maintenance of healthy financial market conditions with financial stability: the exchange rate not to be in any way out of alignment with the fundamentals for a prolonged period of times. The currency must not be imbibed with overvaluation as because overvaluation in that case could act as a catalyst when there will be a run on the currency. The speculators and the private traders in that case will do the massacre for the economy. The liberalization of financial markets should be accompanied by an increase in regulation and strict supervision. Today's financial markets are very very sensitive to new information and also exhibit risks and volatility. Under such circumstances, to meet the emerging challenges before India, a cautious and calibrated approach with enough regulatory and prudential safeguards as well as self-insurance against recent financial crises is urgently called for, before moving towards full CAC. Attention should also be given to maintain the domestic drivers to growth and to avoid running into the classical 'Dutch Disease' situation where non-tradeables become over-priced and erode the competitiveness of the economy in the tradeable sector.

References

Bagchi, Amiya Kumar (2009): "State-led Capitalism and Neoliberalism in A Semi-feudal Society: India 1947-2009", *Presidential Address* delivered at the BEA 29th Conference at University of North Bengal on February 7.

Bhaduri, Amit (2005): *Development with Dignity: A Case for Full Employment*, National Book Trust of India.

Chatterjee, Biswajit and Asim K. Karmakar (1995): "Trade Balance and Domestic Absorption in India: An Eximination of Basic Issues" in S. Murty (ed.), *India's International Trade and Rupee Exchange Rate*, RBSA Publishing, Jaipur-3.

———(1998): "India's Trade Balance and Macroeconomic Policies, in Chatterjee, Biswajit (ed.), *Economic Liberalization in India*, Allied Publishers Pvt. Ltd.

Das, Kaushik (2006): "Issues and Insights—Capital Account Amnesia", *Business Standard*, May 31.

Eichengreen, Barry, Michael Mussa and others (1998): "Capital Account Liberalization—Theoretical and Practical Aspects:, *IMF Occasional Paper* No. 172, IMF, Washington DC.

Habermeier, Karl, (2000): "India's Experience with the Liberalization of Capital Flows Since 1991', *IMF Occasional Paper* (17 May 2000), p. 81.

Karmakar, Asim K. (1994): "External Value of the Rupee and India's Balance of Payments-A Macroeconomic Assessment," *Conference Volume of the IEA.*

———(1998), *Balance of Payments and Economic Development-The Indian Experience During the Period 1951-52 to 1990-91*, Unpublished Ph.D. Dissertation, Jadavpur University.

Kohli, Renu (2005): *Liberalizing Capital Flows: India's Experiences and Policy Issues*, Oxford University Press, New Delhi.

Lahiri, Ashok K. (2009): "Financial Sector: National Priorities Amidst an International Crisis", *EPW*, June 27, Vol. XLIV, Nos. 26 and 27.

Patnaik, Prabhat (2003): "On the Economics of 'Open Economy' De-Industrialization," *V.V. Giri Memorial Lecture* delivered at 45th Annual Conference of the Indian Society of Labour Economics, Jadavpur University, Kolkata, December 16.

Rakshit, Mihir Kanti (2005): "Using Forex Reserves for Infrastructural Investment", *Special Lecture* delivered at the Indian Econometric Society on 20.1.2005 at Jadavpur University.

———(2006): "Some Economics of Capital Account Liberalization", *Special Lecture* delivered at Visva Bharati University at the 26th Annual Conference of Bengal Economic Association.

———(2006): "On Liberalizing Foreign Institutional Investment," *EPW*, March 18-24, Vol. XLI, No. II

Rangarajan, C. and A. Prasad (1999): "Capital Account Liberalization and Controls- Lessons from the East Asian Crisis", *ICRA Bulletin, Money and Finance*, Aprial-June.

Reddy, Y.V. (2006): "Reflections on India's Economic Development," Address to the Council on Foreign Relation, New York, May 12.

Reserve Bank of India: *Report on Currency and Finance, 2001-02, 2002-03, 2003-04.*

Roach, Stephen 92006): 'Global Imbalances Matter More than Ever', *Morgan Stanley Com*, May 5.

Rodrik, Dani (1998): *'Who Needs Capital Account Convertibility'?, Essays in International Finance*, Princeton University, February.

Roy, Mohua, Rekha Misra and Sangita Misra (2006): "A Review of Cross-Country Experience in Capital Account Liberalisation", RBI *Occasional Papers*, Vol. 27, Nos. 1 and 2.

Sen, Pronab, Ashima Goyal and Srinivasan Varadarajan (2006): 'Full Rupee Convertibility: Good, Bad; or Ugly'?, *The Economic Times*, 28.

Sen, Sunanda (2006): 'Drive with Caution', *The Telegraph*, May 9, 2006.

Tarapore, S.S. (2003): *Capital Account Convertibility: Monetary Policy and Reforms*, UBSPD Pvt. Ltd, New Delhi.

Williamson, John, Amitava Krishna Dutta and Others (2006): "Capital Account Convertibility: A Debate," *The Economic Times*, May 13.

Yesuthasen, P. (2006), "Road to Freedom: Capital Account Convertibility," *The Economic Times*, May 10.

5

Open Economy Macroeconomics and Logic of Capital Account Convertibility

DHIRAJ KUMAR BANDYOPADHYAY

ABSTRACT

We know that Capital Account Liberalization (CAL) was undertaken over a period of years in advanced countries, including the euro area, particularly after the breakdown of the Bretton Woods system of fixed exchange rates in the mid-1970s. During the 1980s and 1990s, many of the emerging market economies (EMEs) also undertook capital account liberalization. This was followed by episodes of huge capital inflows into some of these countries the magnitude of which became unmanageable and destabilizing for many EMEs. Based on the cross-country experience in capital account liberalization, especially since the East Asian crisis of 1997, the mainstream thinking both at academic and policy levels has also changed in the recent years.

We also know that economic logic of the liberalization of the capital account for less developed countries (LDCs) such as India is related to the goals of increasing capital inflows in order to increase GDP and growth (and hence contribute to overall economic development) and of smoothing consumption through international borrowing.

Our research question is that—does empirical evidence confirm this logic of capital account liberalization? A substantial increase in capital flows into emerging markets (consisting of LDCs and transitional economies) between early and mid-1990s followed their capital market liberalization. We have studied this phenomenon extensively and the evidence, which suggests that both arguments for capital account liberalization are flawed, can be briefly summarized with our observations.

I. INTRODUCTION

Currency convertibility refers to the freedom to convert the domestic currency into other internationally accepted currencies and vice versa. Convertibility in that sense is the obverse of controls or restrictions on currency transactions. While current account convertibility refers to freedom in respect of payments and transfers of current international transactions, capital account convertibility (CAC) would mean freedom of currency conversion in relation to capital transactions in terms of inflows and outflows.

We know that Capital Account Liberalization (CAL) was undertaken over a period of years in advanced countries, including the Euro area, particularly after the breakdown of the Bretton Woods system of fixed exchange rates in the mid-1970s. During the 1980s and 1990s, many of the emerging market economies (EMEs) also undertook capital account liberalization. This was followed by episodes of huge capital inflows into some of these countries the magnitude of which became unmanageable and destabilizing for many EMEs. Based on the cross-country experience in capital account liberalization, especially since the East Asian crisis of 1997, the mainstream thinking both at academic and policy levels has also changed in the recent years.

Again, historically, capital inflows to the colonies took the form of foreign direct investment (FDI) in mining and plantations and trade credits. Even historically, trade credits and FDI were both very stable components of capital flows. In the next historical episode, inflows took the form of syndicated bank loans to the government. It was much later than other forms of capital inflows, e.g., investment in equity, bank lending to the private sector, occurred. Then the surge of capital inflows to the emerging economies which began in 1989 was supposed to be different from the one in the late 1970s in that in the previous episode almost all the lending was syndicated bank loan, whereas the later inflows were more diversified. What is important, one feature of a financial market that is not fully mature, is that banking is the main form of financial intermediation. And as banks engage in maturity transformation, they are prone to crises. This is also true of the rich countries as well. However, they are able to cope with idiosyncratic shocks better since their production structure tends to be more diversified and banks constitute a smaller proportion of the financial sector.

Against this backdrop, the purpose of our study is to examine the experience of some major emerging market economies (including some developed economies) which went in for capital account liberalization and draw lessons from the experience with particular focus on the circumstances leading to policy reversals of capital account convertibility. Section II essentially deals with a brief comment on the evaluation of capital account liberalization. Section III analyzes the experience of market economies. Section IV attempts a presentation of the macroeconomics logic of capital account convertibility and liberalization policy taken so far by Government of India. Section V concludes with some remarks.

II. EVOLUTION OF CAPITAL ACCOUNT LIBERALIZATION SINCE WORLD WAR II

We know that the post-World War II period from 1945 was marked by imposition of capital controls by most economies. Even the developed countries maintained controls for prolonged periods after World War II, driven by a range of motives including exchange rate policy, monetary policy and tax policy considerations. So, capital flows remained marginal. But capital controls, till the early 1970s, were rather considered as an integral element of the fixed exchange rate regime of the Bretton Woods system.

Again, capital account liberalization became more common after the breakdown of the Bretton Woods system of fixed exchange rates in the mid-1970s. In line with that, several countries gradually switched over to varied forms of floating exchange rates; these countries also liberalized their controls on capital flows. The generalized move towards Capital Account Liberalization (CAL) in the 1980s in the advanced countries coincided with a general shift towards more market-oriented economic policies aimed at achieving non-inflationary growth together with a gradual move towards multilateral framework such as the Organization for Economic Co-operation and Development (OECD) and the European Union (EU). However, barring certain periods of market disruption and speculation in the post-CAL period, there were no cases of serious policy reversals leading to reimposition of capital controls by the advanced economies.

So, many Emerging Market Economies (EMEs) in Latin America and Asia embarked upon capital account liberalization from the early 1980s. Consequently, the volume of capital flows into the developing economies accelerated till the mid-1990s. With the magnitude of capital flows becoming unmanageable and destabilizing for the EMEs and sterilization operations getting increasingly ineffective, some of the EMEs backtracked from the liberal capital account measures and imposed restrictions—both price and non-price-based measures. While some EMEs faced the challenge of managing increased inflows, some other EMEs experienced sudden stops and reversal of flows that led to a series of crises during the mid-1990s. This opened a whole new debate and a plethora of literature on the timing, sequencing and the pace of CAL globally.

As a result of these development, the mainstream thinking in both academic and policy-making circles turned somewhat less enthusiastic about the benefits of capital account liberalization, particularly before meeting several prerequisites in terms of strong macroeconomics policy framework and soundness and efficiency of the financial system and markets. The IMF also shelved its proposal of 1997 for making capital account convertibility as an obligation for its members, and had been following the practice of appropriately advising its members in a country-specific context to follow generally a cautious, gradual and carefully sequenced process of capital account liberalization.

III. AN EXPERIENCE OF EMERGING MARKET ECONOMIES WITH PARTICULAR REFERENCES TO DEVELOPING ECONOMIES

To start with, the decades of 1980s and 1990s saw a range of pressures on developing countries to open up to foreign capital flows triggered by the fast global integration of trade and finance. Malaysia, Indonesia and Thailand and many other market economies like them maintained unrestricted capital accounts in the 1980s and till the mid-1990s. This was followed by episodes of huge capital inflows into these countries particularly in the 1990s, the magnitude of which became unmanageable and destabilizing. Succumbing to the appreciation pressures due to huge inflows, some of these emerging economies reversed the liberal capital account and re-imposed restrictions—both price and non-price-based—around the crisis periods.

The literature on crisis experiences of EMEs shows that the risks of CAL arise mainly from inadequate preparedness before liberalization in terms of domestic and external sector policy consolidation, strengthening of prudential regulation and development of financial markets, including infrastructure, for orderly functioning of these markets.

The Mexican crisis in 1994-95 first drew attention to the volume and velocity of the flows involved in capital account crises in emerging market economies. From the late 1980s to the early 1990s, Mexico liberalized its capital account as part of a larger programme of economic stabilization and reform, internationalization of the stock market and liberalization of FDI. But these elements of liberalization contributed to the eruption of the crisis in December 1994. Though a devaluation of the peso occurred immediately and the peso was allowed to float after a massive loss of international reserves, it did not restore confidence and the peso continued to depreciate sharply, as financial markets were suspicious about Mexico's ability to service its short-term debt.

The East Asian region was characterized by high rates of growth since the 1980s which had accelerated to a range of 7 to 10 per cent in the 1990s accompanied by high investment rates which averaged round 30 per cent through the 1980s (except in the Philippines) and kept well above 30 per cent of GDP and above 40 per cent in Malaysia and Thailand in the 1990s. There were moderate deficits in the general government budget ranging between 0.3 per cent of GDP and 3 per cent of GDP Malaysia recorded deficit of 4 per cent of GDP during the 1980s. But rapidly consolidated its position and moved into fiscal surplus since 1994. Thailand recorded fiscal surpluses all through the 1990s.

We have observed that the East Asian economies faced a serious currency crisis during 1997-99. It began in Thailand without much early warning signals in late June 1997 and afflicted other countries such as Malaysia, Indonesia and South Korea, and lasted upto the last quarter of 1998. It came as a surprise, not only because of the large number of countries affected and the speed of the spreading crisis from one country to another, but also because of the fact that before the crisis many countries had been showing healthy signs: long periods of impressive growth rates, responsible government fiscal policies, and steady investment in human and physical capital. Again, prior to the crisis, there was a boom in private capital flows to emerging markets during the 1990s, which rose to around $300 billion at the time of the East Asian crisis in mid-1997. Some countries allowed entry of this inflow in a completely controlled manner (China, India) while others (e.g., Thailand, Malaysia, Indonesia) had varying degrees of controls. But, the restrictions on outflows also varied among the countries. None of the emerging markets, however, had a fully floating exchange rate. Central banks intervened to restrict movements in exchange rates and most of them sought to keep the exchange rate under an implicit or explicit peg or a band. So, the choice of fixed exchange rate regimes was predicated by the costs and ineffectiveness associated with sterilization, the lack of scope for any further fiscal consolidation, the limit on monetary tightening that would have encouraged further inflows and the erosion in competitiveness which would have occurred under greater exchange rate flexibility.

What is more, fixed nominal exchange rates acted in conjunction with worsening current account imbalances and positive inflation differentials to produce real appreciation of the currencies. Other factors also contributed to currency over-valuation and loss of competitiveness such as the rapid appreciation of the US dollar after 1995, the nominal devaluation of 50 per cent of the Chinese yuan in 994 and the slump in external demand. Now, by taking 1990 as the base year, the real exchange rate appreciated by 19 per cent in Malaysia, 23 per cent in the Philippines, 2 per cent in Thailand and 8 per cent in Indonesia in 1997. The ratio of debt stock (including short-term debt) to reserves, indicating solvency, showed that except Indonesia and the Philippines for whom this ratio was 267 per cent and 166 per cent, respectively, other Asian economies were well below 100 per cent. The share of short-term debt to total debt varied between 3 per cent (in Philippines) and 32 per cent (in Thailand). In retrospect, the key weaknesses were the large inflow of short-term capital and the fact that most of the affected countries had high current account deficit and overvalued exchange rates.

The crisis left a trace of heavy economic and social costs. These Asian economies saw an overall decline in 1998. Gross Domestic Product (GDP) in 1998 contracted almost 6 per cent in Korea, 8 per cent in Thailand and 7 per cent in Malaysia. Social unrest and political uncertainty compounded the economic and financial dislocations in Indonesia to reduce real GDP by almost 14 per cent.

IV. MACROECONOMIC LOGIC OF LIBERALIZATION

We know that the economic logic of the liberalization of the capital account for less developed countries (LDCs) such as India related to the goals of increasing capital inflows in order to increase GDP and growth (and hence contribute to overall economic development) and of smoothing consumption through international borrowing.

We argue that the output-enhancing effect of capital

account liberalization can be seen from a simple textbook model in which one good is produced in two countries with two factors of production—'capital' and 'labour', with given technology under conditions of diminishing returns to each factor. Let us suppose that the only difference between the two countries is that one—a developed country, DC—has a higher stock of capital than the other, an LDC. Now, under the assumption of perfect competition, but with labour and capital immobile between the two countries, the return to capital or the rental rate—will be higher in the LDC than in the DC. So, if capital is allowed to move from the low-rental country to the high-rental country in search of higher returns, it will move from the rich country to the poor country, lowering its cost of capital, and adding to its production and income after paying the rent or return to capital to the rich country. Therefore, to the extent that the accumulation of capital leads to higher growth, such international capital flows increase growth in LDCs.

Next, the consumption-stabilizing impact can be shown with another simple model in which a country with a representative agent can borrow or lend at a given world interest rate. Let us suppose that the representative individual receives a stream of income which is subject to exogenous fluctuations. If consumption exhibits diminishing marginal utility, the individual will be able to increase its inter-temporal utility if it can participate in the international capital market and stabilize consumption.

Empirical Validity of International Capital Flow and Liberalization

Our research question is that—does empirical evidence confirm this logic of capital account liberalization? A substantial increase in capital flows into emerging markets (consisting of LDCs and transitional economies) in the early and mid-1990s followed their capital market liberalization. We have studied this phenomenon extensively and the evidence, which suggests that both arguments for capital account liberalization are flawed, can be briefly summarized with our observations.

At first, for reasonably long periods of time, and

especially in recent years, there has been a reverse net transfer of financial resources from LDCs to rich countries. For instance, from 1997 onwards net transfers to LDCs have been negative, increasing from $5.2 billion in 1997 to over $350 billion in 2004, explained by a combination of low levels of net financial flows and the accumulation of foreign exchange reserves.

Secondly, episodes of booms in capital inflows, especially short-term capital flows, end abruptly and turn into sharp outflows.

Thirdly, capital flows to emerging markets have been pro-cyclical, with large inflows during periods of economic expansion and outflows during recessions. Further, fiscal and monetary policies tend to be pro-cyclical in LDCs and therefore exacerbate their business cycles.

Fourthly, most episodes of interrelated banking and currency crises in emerging markets have been preceded by financial liberalization and increased access to foreign capital markets.

These findings regarding capital market liberalization and capital flows, especially portfolio investment and hot money flows, are well known and widely recognized.

Asymmetric Information and Instability in the Financial System

Now the question is why is the logic of capital market liberalization at odds with the actual experience of LDCs? We argue that it is flawed because it fails to come to grips with some fundamental features of reality of which the most important arguably relates to information.

Now, contrary to the assumption of perfect information in the standard model, information is imperfect in capital markets. Without deviating from the standard neoclassical assumption of optimizing agents, models with asymmetric information produce results which are far more consistent with reality. If lenders do not know exactly what borrowers do with borrowed funds and can only observe outcomes of their activity, while borrowers know what they are doing, we have the problem of asymmetric information, and lenders will require collateral to ensure that borrowers do not wilfully default. The implication of this is that borrowers in rich countries who have higher initial endowments of capital will be able to borrow more than those in poor countries because they can put up collateral to overcome moral hazard problems, while in poor countries they are less able to do so. Therefore, this implies that capital will flow from poor to rich countries, making rich countries even richer resulting in a process of uneven development. Then the borrowers in poor countries will not be able to borrow what they want to causing rationing which become tighter when poor countries experience bad times, implying that capital flows to poor countries will be pro-cyclical and not stabilize their consumption.

Now, what is interesting is that similar implications emerge from Keynes' (1936) view of asset markets, in which investors are faced with fundamental uncertainty; they simply do not know the returns they can expect from their investments. In such a situation they form expectations of the future, knowing fully well that these expectations are built on flimsy foundations. In forming these expectations they may follow conventions, such as following the lead of others, which gives rise to herd mentality, and such conventions and expectations are likely to be subject to large changes in reaction to new information. At certain times business optimism is high, and that makes firms invest more, and this expansion results in an increase in aggregate demand which further fuels investment. This is possible because, unlike the neo-classical full employment model, the economy has unemployed resources. As the expansion proceeds, some firms may feel overextended and suddenly lose their confidence, and investment is curtailed, resulting in a reverse process of contraction and rising unemployment. Stock markets also add to the instability.

Keynes' ideas have been extended and refined by post-Keynesian economists, most notably Minsky (1982), who analysed how the expectations of firms as borrowers and banks as lenders would change and interact. During the expansion firms borrow more and this leads them to become more indebted. Increased indebtedness leads lenders and borrowers to perceive greater risks, which induce lenders to increase the interest rate and borrowers to cut down on borrowing and investment. Then this decline in investment reduces aggregate demand in the standard Keynesian manner and results in a decline in profits which, along with the increase in interest rates leads to a downward spiral. Now, matters can be exacerbated when funds flow into real estate and stock markets. Herd mentality can lead to bubbles in these markets during the expansion, and when the bubbles inevitably burst, the price of assets (including those serving as collateral) tumble, which aggravates the financial positions of borrowers and lenders, leading to sharp reductions in lending and economic activity, as well as to bankruptcies. Keynes and Minsky were mainly discussing the financial markets within advanced capitalist economies, in which central banks can stabilize the economy but matters are more complicated when we turn to international financial markets and LDCs.

Now, extending the analysis to international markets complicates matters for a number of reasons, including the following:

First, the problems of uncertainty and asymmetric information are greater because market participants have less knowledge about situations and borrowers in distant countries. Lenders are therefore more likely to have their expectations built on flimsy foundations, exhibit more of a herd mentality, and rely more on conventions which are subject to sudden changes. Second, the fact that international markets operate with different currencies create additional sources of instability. During the boom, currency appreciation in borrower nations can lead to greater euphoria, and because loans have to be paid back in the currencies of lender nations, when loans are recalled during the downswing, currency depreciation can make it more difficult for borrowers to pay back loans. (Exchange rate fluctuations can in theory stabilize the market, but in practice have been found to amplify the lending cycles). Third, because of contagion effects across borders, for instance because foreign banks who suffer losses in one country can call back loans to another country, problems arising in one country can be transferred to other countries, introducing additional sources of instability. Fourth, since financial capital can move from one country to another, changes in the supply of finance to an economy can be greater than in a closed economy. Finally, the absence of a world central bank and the absence of monetary authorities that can regulate the amount of liquidity reduce the chances of containing the problem. In fact, the IMF, the closest thing to a world central bank, exacerbates the instability, deepening the bust by imposing austerity measures and other contractionary policies on borrowing countries, and by encouraging the imprudent lending boom by being ready to bail out lenders when financial crises occur.

LDCs, and particularly India are prone to these problems while rich countries seldom experience currency crises. The small size of their financial markets—especially stock and currency markets—implies that a given change in capital flows has a large proportional effect on these markets. Poor prudential regulation and supervision of financial institutions, and the inexperience of financial agents in evaluating risks make them less able to reduce the instability of capital flows. Their thin securities markets reduce the ability of their monetary authorities to follow counter-cyclical policies which could dampen the fluctuations.

V. CONCLUDING REMARKS

Unstable capital flows (although some components, such as foreign direct investment may be less unstable than others) can be expected to have adverse consequences on economic growth and social indicators in LDCs and particularly for India where GDP growth so far achieved is by no means a long-run achievement (Table 1). Still, India has not been running into long-run favourable balance on current account. The calculated Table shows that the Debt-GDP ratios is still deplorable. The growth of Indian economy is not inclusive, rather it is exclusive in nature. The financial sector in this environment will not be able to absorb shocks which may be generated exogenously or endogenously in the Indian financial system and which may arise particularly through foreign institutional investment and short-term capital inflow. The major part of the Indian foreign exchange reserve

TABLE 1

Macroeconomic Aggregates of India

Year	Real GDP growth (%)	Invest-ment/ GDP	Infla-tion (%)	Current Account Balance (% of GDP)	Current receipts to GDP (%)	Reserves (US $ billion)	Reserves/ Imports (Months)	Exchange rates app.(+)/ {Dep.(-)} (period average)	Debt service ratio (%)	Budge-tary balance/ GDP (%)	Exports/ GDP (%)	FDI/ GDP (%)
1	2	3	4	5	6	7	8	9	10	11	12	13
1995	7.6	24.4	10.2	-1.6	13.1	17.9	5.1	-3.3	25.9	-5.1	11.0	0.6
1996	7.5	22.8	9.0	-1.5	13.9	20.2	5.0	-8.5	26.2	-4.9	10.6	0.6
1997	5.0	21.7	7.2	-0.7	14.4	24.7	5.9	-2.4	23.0	-5.8	10.9	0.9
1998	6.0	21.5	13.2	-1.7	13.7	27.3	6.6	-12.0	19.5	-6.5	11.2	0.6
1999	7.0	21.8	4.7	-0.7	14.5	32.7	7.8	-4.2	18.8	-5.3	11.8	0.5
2000	5.3	22.0	4.0	-1.0	16.3	37.9	7.6	-4.2	17.1	-5.6	13.9	0.8
2001	4.1	22.0	3.8	0.3	16.8	45.9	9.7	-4.8	16.2	-6.2	13.5	1.1
2002	4.2	22.2	4.3	1.4	17.9	67.7	13.4	-2.9	13.7	-5.9	15.3	1.1
2003	7.2	22.7	3.8	1.1	18.5	98.9	15.7	4.4	16.0	-4.5	14.9	0.8

2004	8.1	23.7	3.8	1.7	22.0	126.6	14.3	2.8	16.3	-4.0	19.1	0.8
2005	8.3		4.2			131.9	10.6	2.8				

Calculate from:

(i) World Economic Outlook;

(ii) World Bank Online Database;

(iii) World Economic Outlook and World Bank Online Database;

(iv) International Financial Statistics, IMA; and

(v) International Financial Statistics and IMF Article IV Documents.

constitutes the short-term capital inflow so far ensured by official account (Table 1). Judging by the European experience after the World war II, it takes about 30 years for a country which starts the process of liberalization and financial integration to move to capital account convertibility. That is why we argue that the proposed full capital account convertibility as well as liberalization is at least, in the perspective of world financial system, about 10 to 5 years premature to implement in India.

References

Datta, Amitava Krishna (2006), 'Flawed Logic of Capital Account Liberalisation,' *Economic and Political Weekly*, May, p. 13.

Kaminsky, Graciela and Carmen, Reinhard (1999), 'The Twin Crises: The Causes of Banking and Balance of Payments Problems', *American Economic Review*, 89(3), June, pp. 473-500.

Keynes, John Maynard (1936), *The General Theory of Employment, Interest and Money*, Macmillan, London.

Minsky, Hyman (1982), *Can 'It' Happen Again?*, Armond, K.E. Sharpe, New York.

Nayyar, Deepak (2002). 'Capital Controls and the World Financial Authority: What Can We Learn from the Indian Experience?' in J. Eatwell and L. Taylor (eds.), *International Capital Markets*, Oxford University Press, Oxford.

Rakshit, Mihir (2006), 'On Liberalising Foreign Institutional Investments,' *Economic and Political Weekly*, March 18, pp. 991-98.

Reserve Bank of India Bulletin, Various issues.

Reserve Bank of India (2006), *Report of the Committee on Fuller Capital Account Convertibility*, Mumbai.

Stiglitz, Joseph E. (2002), *Globalization and Its Discontents*, W.W. Norton, New York.

6

Liberalization of Capital Account in India: An Overview

JAYDEB SARKHEL AND CHANCHAL CHATTERJEE

ABSTRACT

In the realm of rapid globalization, the global integration of financial markets has become an important issue in the world of finance. Full convertibility of rupee on capital account is an important step towards such global integration. Capital Account Convertibility (CAC) implies that there would be no controls on the two-way movement of international capital and on their end-use except in cases of transactions which are undesirable in nature. Such Capital Account Convertibility can be expected to bring some advantages to the nation. But at the same time, some precautionary steps in respect of several important sectors of the economy are to be taken before implementing the system of full capital mobility with a view to make this approach ever successful. In this backdrop, an attempt has been made in the present article to explain different issues of Capital Account Convertibility (CAC) in India.

I INTRODUCTION

With rapid globalization, the integration of financial markets globally has become an important issue in the world of finance. Full convertibility of capital account transactions is an important step towards such global integration of financial markets. At the end of December, 1996, the international Monetary Fund (IMF) classified 57 nations as not having restrictions on payment for capital account transactions by conducting a survey of capital controls in 155 developing countries. India is now in a debating stage regarding the issue of whether to go for full capital mobility. The Reserve Bank of India (RBI), on February 28, 1997, appointed a committee on Capital Account Convertibility (CAC) under the Chairmanship of S.S. Tarapore. The committee, more popularly known as Tarapore Committee, in its report, mentioned some benefits expected to flow from CAC. It also mentioned some pre-conditions before adopting CAC in respect of fiscal consolidation, inflation rate, financial sector reforms, exchange rate policy, balance of payments (BOP), etc. The committee also suggested that the CAC should be implemented in a phased manner over a period of three years starting with 1997-98. Capital Account Convertibility (CAC) refers to the freedom or liberty to convert local/domestic financial assets into foreign financial assets and *vice-versa* at market determined rates of exchange. It is associated with changes of ownership in domestic/foreign financial assets and liabilities and embodies the creation and settlement of claims on, or by the rest of the world. CAC also implies that there would be no government controls, regulations, etc. on the movement of international capital and on their ultimate use except in cases of transactions that are undesirable in nature. India has already made progressive liberalization of current account transactions and it is also important to mention that the question of CAC is a natural corollary of current account convertibility. In this article, an effort has been made to give a brief account of this issue (CAC). This paper has also made an attempt to discuss several issues associated with CAC such as the advantages expected from CAC, its impact on different sectors of the economy, the pre-conditions to be fulfilled or the precautions to be taken before going to full capital account convertibility.

The present article has been organized in six separate sections. The next section (Section II) explains the benefits or advantages expected to flow from free capital mobility. The impact of CAC on different sectors of the economy has been highlighted in the Section III. Section IV has been devoted to the brief discussion of international experience with a free capital mobility. The preconditions which are to be fulfilled before going to free Capital Account Convertibility have also been summarized in Section V and finally the last Section VI deals with the concluding remarks.

II. BENEFITS ARISING FROM CAC

The following benefits are expected to arise from a more open capital account: CAC allows availability of a larger amount of foreign capital to supplement domestic resources and thereby higher growth, improved access to global financial markets, reduction in costs of capital, etc. can be achieved.

Another argument in favour of CAC is that, the residents can register gains from trade in international financial assets as CAC allows them to hold a globally diversified portfolio that helps to reduce the volatility of income streams and wealth of domestic shocks. Nay, it also enables lower funding costs for borrowers and allows savers' prospects of higher returns.

Allocational efficiency is improved as a consequence of dynamic gains arising from financial integration which in turn, stimulates innovation and improves productivity.

The free mobility of capital provides an impetus to domestic tax regimes to rationalize and converse to international and global framework of taxation. This facilitates the removal of inducements for domestic agents toward tax evasion as well as capital flight.

CAC plays an important role in maintaining discipline in domestic policies; it enhances the effectiveness of fiscal policy by reducing real interest rates for public sector borrowing, brings about an optimal combination of taxes and also reduce crowding out effects of access of funds. In a nutshell, prudent fiscal policy plays an important role in canalizing capital flows more and more to productive sectors of the economy.

III. IMPACT OF CAC ON THE ECONOMY

India's move towards Capital Account Convertibility is expected to have significant impact on various sectors of the economy, such as Banks and Financial Institutions, Stock Exchanges, Exchange rates, etc. A brief explanation of such impact of CAC is shown below:

On investment and GDP: Due to the two-way movement of capital and the increased inflow of capital into the economy either in the form of FDI or Portfolio Investment by Foreign Institutional Investors (FIIs), interest rates may be expected to decline considerably. As a consequence of this, the investment and GDP growth rate are presumed to rise which would facilitate the general economic development of the country.

On Banks and Financial Institutions: Due to large inflow of capital, the magnitude of business of banks would be enhanced but their "spreads" will be squeezed. The strategy of corporate restructuring through mergers and consolidation may become necessary especially for small banks for maintaining and ensuring their survival, existence and growth in the arena of stiff competition. If rupee slides down significantly, banks engaged in borrowing from overseas will face problem. Active intervention on the part of the RBI and proper precautions for meeting such contingencies on the part of the banks are essential. On the other side of the coin, banks will have an opportunity of borrowing foreign capital at relatively low costs. However, for reducing NPAs and for ensuring their survival and growth, banks will have to enhance their efficiency, reduce operating costs, modernize management, introduce latest information technology, for raising productivity, etc. Financial Institutions may not be in an advantageous position if they are treated at par with banks. If they have to operate within the boundary of SLR requirement and priority sector lending, their profitability may be affected.

On Stock Exchanges

As a consequence of CAC, the inflows are expected to increase in the stock markets and investment will rise if such funds are invested in infrastructure industries like steel, cement, bridges and roads, telecom and other constructions, etc. Moreover, liquidity in the stock markets is likely to increase and offer a wide range of choice to the investor. However, in order to meet the proposed challenges of CAC, stock exchanges are to be prepared suitably. First, market efficiency should be improved by incorporating updated and modern valuation techniques, and sophisticated information technology. Secondly, the accounting and disclosure norms should be of international standards. Thirdly, with a view to reduce volatility and enhance liquidity in the stock markets, a wide range of financial derivatives like futures options, etc. should be introduced. Transparency of transactions should be ensured in the stock exchanges.

IV. INTERNATIONAL EXPERIENCE WITH FREE CAPITAL MOBILITY

So far as the Committee on CAC (i.e., Tarapore Committee) is concerned, the Committee made a study of the experiences of ten countries after introducing CAC. Of these, four countries, viz. Argentina, Indonesia, Malaysia and New Zealand are classified by the IMF as not having restrictions on CAC. The other six nations namely, Chile, Mexico, Korea, Thailand, Philippines and South Africa have registered varied experiences on the issue of capital account liberalization. However, a brief picture of the experiences of some of these countries is depicted below:

In Argentina, CAC has been implemented in two stages, i.e. in 1976-81 and 1989-91. The first phase of CAC was made even though the economy was suffering from several drawbacks such as severe macroeconomic disequilibrium with shortage of foreign exchange, high rate of inflation, negative net foreign exchange reserves, etc. In the next phase, the country registered fiscal discipline, inflation control, strengthening the BoP situation and by reporting surplus in the current account and building up foreign exchange reserves. The Currency Board and the Law of Convertibility also came into being in 1991.

Indonesia gathered a unique experience with CAC. Here the open capital account was established despite weak initial conditions and the capital account was liberalized before the current account. It, however, hampered the economic performance of the nation significantly. The domestic saving rate had declined and even reported negative in 1966-67, BoP deteriorated, foreign exchange reserves were totally eroded, and inflation rate was well above 100% up to 1988. Thereafter, the country benefited from oil boom during the seventies. CAC played a vital role in accelerating financial and real sector reforms and facilitated the improvement of confidence level among global investors.

Mexico's step towards liberalization of capital account was made in-an environment of stability and growth. Here the liberalization of capital account has been undertaken selectively since 1989. With such type of liberalization, the country has become successful in making significant progress in financial sector reforms, controlling the rate of inflation and also fiscal consolidation desirably.

Thailand's approach towards CAC was initiated in the nineties when it emerged as a rapidly growing industrializing economy. Due to strong capital flows, the overall BoP registered a surplus but a deficit balance had occurred in the current account. In a nutshell, the constraints associated with infrastructural development, increasing overvaluation due to the fixed exchange rate, significant deficit in the current account of the country's BOP represent the non-existence of strong signals in Thailand's approach towards free capital mobility.

V. PRECONDITIONS TO BE FULFILLED FOR CAC

Before making a final move towards opening up of the capital account fully, the concerned authority(s) should devote due attention to some sensitive, significant as well as important priority areas with a view to make this approach successful in the overall interest of the nation. In other words, certain pre-conditions are necessarily required to be fulfilled before taking the final step towards CAC. Some important signposts for CAC are pointed out one by one:

Fiscal Consolidation

The proportion of Gross Fiscal Deficit (GFD) to GDP should be reduced over time by taking appropriate measures. The fiscal deficit of the centre as well as the states should be reduced considerably. Moreover, the amount procured through the technique of fresh borrowing should not be used for financing the amortization of market loans of the government. Not only that, as per the recommendation of the Tenth Finance Commission, a consolidated sinking fund (CSF) for public debt should be established which is an important element of fiscal consolidation. Apart from these, globally comparable procedures for fiscal accounting should be implemented in order to bring transparency. A system of fiscal transparency should be established like New Zealand's Fiscal Responsibility Act.

Control of Inflation Rate

Appropriate and effective measures should be made to generate a specific commitment on the rate of inflation. A medium-term inflation mandate should be approved by Parliament and the authority of altering it should be vested in the Parliament alone. There should, however, be clear and unambiguous guidelines indicating the circumstances under which the mandate could be altered. Moreover, the Central Bank should be given liberty in using the instruments at its command for attaining the medium-term inflation target.

Reforms of the Financial Sector

A well prepared financial system should be developed so as to handle the structural changes that are expected to emerge from the introduction of CAC. Steps should be taken to strengthen the financial system and bring transparency in the system. The country should ensure full deregulation of the interest rates without having any formal or informal controls. Moreover, effective as well as drastic measures should be undertaken with a view to reduce the quantum of NPAs of banks (especially public sector banks) gradually within a specific time period. Action should be taken to reduce the CRR of banks progressively.

Apart from these, proper attention should also be given to the management of some important indicators. Due attention towards such ingredients is another vital pre-condition for CAC. These factors are stated below briefly:

Exchange Rate Policy: Exchange rate flexibility is another necessary ingredient for maintaining viability of free capital mobility. A regime of flexibility is not free from bottlenecks, but is preferable to a fixed exchange rate regime in a situation of moving toward CAC. In this connection, it should also be mentioned that the RBI should have a Monitoring Exchange Rate Band around the normal Real Effective Exchange Rate (REER) and the RBI should not intervene when the REER does not exceed the band. The management of exchange rate policy is very much vital for bringing transparency in introducing CAC.

Adequate Foreign Exchange Reserves: Capital flows arising out of free capital mobility would have a significant impact on the balance of payments of the country. The traditional indicators in terms of import cover cannot be expected to provide a sound indicator of the adequacy of reserves. Hence, an adequate volume of foreign exchange reserves should always be maintained and it should be equal to at least six months of imports.

VI. CONCLUSION

Whether capital account transactions in India should be entirely liberalized or not, is an academic question. The country's move towards CAC is expected to offer some advantages to the nation. But at the same time, this approach is not totally free from bottlenecks or risks. If, however, this approach is finally undertaken, some pre-conditions as mentioned earlier should be fulfilled duly in order to reduce risks associated with this step. Not only that, the country should implement this approach (i.e., free capital mobility) in a phased manner through some stages of specific period of time. The success or failure arising out of such decision of CAC should be evaluated scientifically. Such periodic assessment is expected to help the nation in measuring progress towards the attainment of the signposts stipulated for the relevant time period. For making the country's move towards CAC successful, an effective supervisory regime is essential because it would help the nation in pinpointing the warning signals and monitoring the weaker entities properly. Moreover, the Risk Management System, updated Management Information System, etc. are also essential for effective implementation as well as management of this approach. Finally, the intimate and honest participation of the talented and expert individuals, banks and financial institutions is desirable for making India's movement towards Capital Account Convertibility successful.

References

Dutt, A.K. (2006): "Flawed Logic of Capital Account Liberalization", *Economic and Political Weekly*, May 13.

Tarapore Committee (1997): *Report of the Committee on Capital Account Convertibility*, Reserve Bank of India, Mumbai.

Sen, P. (2006): "Case against Rushing into Full Capital Account Convertibility", *Economic and Political Weekly*, May, 13.

Bhagwati, Jagdish (2004): *In Defense of Globalization*, Oxford University Press, Oxford.

7

Walking the Road of Capital Account Convertibility: Too Risky for India?

GAGARI CHAKRABARTI

ABSTRACT

Proponents of market economics take capital account convertibility to be desirable and inevitable as it is a part of the inexorable process of globalization. However, while direct benefits of capital account convertibility cannot be denied, moving towards it is accompanied by substantial risks, particularly for the developing countries. Its benefits depend upon the achievement of certain preconditions and sequencing patterns and an orderly liberalization procedure. The opening up of the capital account is a more complicated procedure than often thought. After the Asian crisis, estimate of potential cost of capital account liberalization has increased and the emphasis has shifted to caution. It is desirable to opt for a gradual approach so that it can be embedded in the overall reform process. In this light, the present paper discusses the case for capital account convertibility in India. Until recently, IMF classified India as "largely liberalized country" and now she is thriving to dismantle remaining obstacles to full capital mobility. However, with some of the preconditions set by the Tarapore Committee yet to be met, issue of throwing open the capital account might be fraught with risk. A cautious approach is thus vital.

I. INTRODUCTION

Capital market liberalization is viewed as part of a broader process of financial liberalization and international economic integration. The proponents of market economics argue that "capital account liberalization is an inevitable step on the path to international development, which cannot be avoided and should be embraced" (*Fischer*, 1998). Over the years, the miraculous growth rates in advanced countries, in OECD or in East Asian countries, have been attributed to the policy of combining capital account convertibility (CAC) with export-led growth. On the contrary, the developing countries' growth with capital controls (in the form of exchange rate controls, maintaining dual exchange rate or taxes on short-term capital flow) and import substitution strategy stagnated. By 1995, while almost all industrial countries had implemented CAC, developing countries mostly retained capital control. More recently, most of them (except South Asia and China) have moved fairly rapidly to dismantle capital control despite initially weak macroeconomic conditions.

India joined this bandwagon quite recently. Thus far, Indian capital account has remained 'largely liberalized' according to IMF classification. Recently, there has been substantial debate on whether to dismantle the remaining obstacles to full capital mobility. However, this might be coupled with risk. Over the years, spates of currency crises and the resulting capital flow reversals plunged the economies that had enjoyed the benefit of full capital mobility into deep economic crisis. After the East Asian crisis, the estimate of the potential cost of liberalization has changed with emphasis shifted to caution. In this light, India's recent rush towards CAC might turn out to be premature and risky. That is the area what this paper would explore.

II. CAPITAL ACCOUNT CONVERTIBILITY: BENEFITS FOR DEVELOPING COUNTRIES

Tarapore Committee (1997) defines CAC as "the

freedom to convert local financial assets into foreign financial assets and *vice-versa* at market determined rates of exchange". Thus, CAC implies complete mobility of capital across countries. CAC is favoured on several grounds (*Dooley*, 1996; *Fisher*, 1998). Like free trade, it leads to efficient resource allocation and welfare maximization. CAC gives resource constrained developing countries an access to global savings pool. Bridging the savings-investment gap could lead to improved productivity and growth. Moreover, international diversification of portfolio promotes risk spreading and maximizes risk-adjusted returns. It further brings forth intertemporal smoothing of consumption pattern. Most importantly, the fear of capital flow reversal could restrict use of imprudent domestic policies in a regime with capital mobility.

However, in reality international trade in financial asset is marked by market failure or domestic distortion arising from asymmetric information and/or non-information factors (*Karunaratne*, 2001). With such distortions, CAC may not be the first best policy and could even reduce welfare. Information asymmetry manifests itself in various distortions such as adverse selection where lenders with less information than the borrowers about the profitability of any project, might end up choosing a non-viable project. Often the investors take up undue risks that are passed onto some third party such as tax payers, thereby creating a problem of moral hazard. Alternatively, there might be herd behaviour where decisions are not based on fundamentals. Although all financial markets are subject to some degree of asymmetric information (*Eichengreen et al.*, 1999), adverse impacts of these might be removed through development of proper institutional mechanism (*Karunaratne*, 2001).

Presence of non-information distortions might lead to reverse capital flight with CAC. CAC with trade distortion might provoke adoption of capital-intensive technology in labour abundant developing nations (*Dooley*, 1996). CAC could complicate the conduct of macroeconomic policy, essentially by constraining the level of the domestic interest rate. Moreover, it could reduce the existing narrow tax base of the developing countries. It is difficult to tax overseas earnings, and this makes it attractive to countries to prohibit the export of domestic capital (*Razin and Sadka,* 1991). Empirical evidence reveals that countries with capital controls exhibit relatively high inflation (*Dooley,* 1996) and lower real interest rates. CAC therefore either increases explicit tax rates or reduces government expenditure (*Giovannini and de Melo,* 1993).

With CAC, a transition to floating exchange rate is preferred. However, such transition requires a degree of central bank independence which developing countries can hardly afford. Further, growth enhancing effect of CAC is not yet proved empirically for developing nations (*Rodrik,* 1998).

Moreover, while implementing CAC, issues of speed and sequencing of the liberalization process are important (*Fisher,* 1998). *McKinnon* (1973) wanted CAC not to precede current account convertibility. Since asset markets react more speedily to liberalization than the commodity market, the resulting inflow of capital would lead to appreciation of real exchange rate eroding the benefits of trade liberalization of current account convertibility process. An antithetical view, however, assures that such inflow of funds might not be inflationary or lead to exchange rate appreciation (*Karunaratne,* 2001). 'Any question of sequencing is not one of trade *versus* capital, but rather of "clean-up" followed by opening' (*Dornbusch,* 1998).

The assurance that CAC would attract foreign direct investment (FDI) and portfolio investment (FPI) to help developing nations raise growth rates and reduce poverty is debatable. Openness to FPI offers fewer benefits and imparts greater costs than does openness to FDI. However, FDI and FPI are not correlated and many of the benefits of access to FDI can be obtained without CAC. CAC could stimulate FDI only after proper institution-building and goods market liberalization. (*Gilbert et al.,* 2000). Thus, while the direct benefits of CAC cannot be refuted, these are likely to be effective only when other reforms are at least in progress. An anatomy of international experience with CAC could make things clear.

III. INTERNATIONAL EXPERIENCE WITH CAPITAL ACCOUNT CONVERTIBILITY

Financial world has witnessed spates of currency crisis generated by sudden reversal in capital flow arising from change in market sentiments. Such 'casino economy' (*Karunaratne,* 2001) has been so disruptive from the standpoint of both growth and welfare that economists' emphasis has shifted to caution.

Three generations model are used to analyse global experience with CAC. These are based on experiences of the countries that suffered from currency crisis in the past The First generation model is based on the currency crisis of the Latin American countries in late seventies. Such models isolate worsening of macroeconomic fundamentals as root cause of reverse capital flight and collapse of exchange rate peg. Second generation model owes its origin to the Mexican problem in 1994. It is some sort of multiple equilibria model based on rational self-fulfilling expectations where such expectations switch from a good equilibrium to a bad equilibrium depending on market sentiment. Here, after comparing the cost of maintaining the peg with the potential cost of devaluation, the peg is abandoned for short-term macroeconomic gains. Third generation models were introduced particularly to analyse the Asian currency crisis that the other two models could not explain. The first version of this model emphasises that implicit government guarantee encouraged financial intermediaries to overborrow in unhedged foreign currency: a typical moral hazard problem. Huge investments in risky real estate and asset purchases led to asset price bubble. Bursting of bubble triggered capital outflow. In the second version, with implicit guarantee and in absence of prudential regulation in the banking and financial system and a weak corporate sector, funds were channelled into risky ventures. A liquidity crisis generated by some exogenous shock created panic and herd behaviour among the investors. With a craze to withdraw funds, a liquidity crisis might develop leading to an insolvency crisis enhancing reversal of capital flow further.

IV. LESSONS FROM PAST EXPERIENCE—WHEN CAC IS POSSIBLE?

The most important lesson that these spates of currency crises offer is that perhaps capital account liberalization in absence of prudential framework would lead to an external crisis (*Goldstein,* 1998; *Griffith-Jones, Williamson and Gottschalk,* 2005). To reap full advantage of CAC domestic financial sector reforms and corporate financial structure reforms to cope with capital inflow and outflow are vital. A movement away from quantitative restriction to market determined interest rates, prudential norms and adequate monitoring, and development of government securities market are necessary.

CAC should be preceded by the establishment of sound macroeconomic fundamentals with emphasis on fiscal sustainability, suitable monetary policy and price stability. Fiscal and monetary policies should ensure that volatility of capital flows is minimised. This requires low inflation, balanced budget and an independent central bank. Large budget deficit resulting in high real interest rate would attract inflows leading to currency appreciation. With fixed exchange rates this inflow could increase nominal money supply generating inflation. Sterilization through open market operation would require some depth in money market Moreover, it increases government debt held by residents and increases the interest cost and current account deficit might become unsustainable. Anticipation of such an eventuality could lead to capital outflows. Sterilization through usual route would require maintaining cash reserve ratio in line with international level.

With CAC flexible exchange rates are absolutely vital. Fixed exchange rates do not allow for inflation differentials and convert returns into foreign currencies one-for-one. With implicit guarantee, fixed exchange rate increases inflows with the borrowing denominated in the foreign currency, which may then be lent to the non-traded goods sector. If an exchange rate crisis is feared, market participants move out of the domestic currency depleting the foreign exchange reserves of the central bank and leading to breakdown of the fixed exchange rate regime. This creates a problem in the banking sector where balance sheets deteriorate in terms of the foreign currency. Central bank's attempt to protect the peg by raising interest rates might be unsuccessful (*Sen*, 2006). With these pros and cons in mind a case for CAC in India will now be examined.

V. CAPITAL ACCOUNT CONVERTIBILITY: CASE FOR INDIA

India's move towards CAC was a part of her liberalization process that started in 1991. Rupee was made convertible on current account in 1994. Tarapore Committee set up by the RBI laid the "road map" to CAC in 1997. The Committee recommended a three-year time frame for CAC by 1999-2000 and highlighted necessary preconditions as follows:

- Reduction of gross fiscal deficit to GDP ratio from a budgeted 4.5% in 1997-98 to 3.5% in 1999-2000.
- Setting up of a consolidated sinking fund to meet government's debt repayment needs, financed by RBI's profit transfer to the government and disinvestment proceeds.
- Inflation rate to remain at an average 3-5% for the 3-year period 1997-2000.
- Reduction of gross NPAs of the public sector banking system to 5% by 2000. At the same time, average effective CRR needs to be brought down to 3%.
- RBI should have a Monitoring Exchange Rate Band of plus minus 5% around a neutral Real Effective Exchange Rate.
- Redesigning of external sector policies to increase receipts to GDP ratio and curtail the debt servicing ratio from 25% to 20%. The Committee recommended a phased liberalization of capital controls over the three year period.
- Indian Joint Venture/Wholly Owned Subsidiaries should be allowed to invest up to $50 million in ventures abroad at the level of the Authorised

Dealers (ADs) in Phase I with transparent and comprehensive guidelines set out by the RBI. The existing requirement of repatriation of the invested amount within a period of 5 years may be removed.

- o Exchange earners may be allowed 100% retention of earnings in Exchange Earners' Foreign Currency accounts with complete flexibility in operation including cheque writing facility in Phase I.
- o Individual residents may be allowed to invest in assets in financial market abroad up to $25,000 in Phase I with progressive increase to $50,000 in Phase II and $100,000 in Phase Ill. Similar limits may be allowed for non-residents out of their non-repatriable assets in India.
- o SEBI registered Indian investors may be allowed to set funds for investments abroad subject to overall limits of $500 million in Phase I, $1 billion in Phase II and $2 billion in Phase III.
- o Banks may be allowed more liberal limits for borrowings from abroad and deployment of funds outside India. Borrowings may be subject to an overall limit of 50% of unimpaired Tier I capital in Phase I, 75% in Phase II and 100% in Phase III.
- o Foreign direct and portfolio investment and disinvestment should be governed by comprehensive and transparent guidelines, and prior RBI approval at various stages may be dispensed with subject to reporting by ADs.
- o Participants on the spot market could operate in the forward markets: all Indian Financial Institutions (FIs) fulfilling requisite criteria could become full-fledged ADs; currency futures may be introduced; participation in money markets may be widened, market segmentation removed and interest rates deregulated; the RBI should withdraw from the primary market in Government securities; the role of primary and satellite dealers should be increased; fiscal incentives should be provided for individuals

investing in Government securities; the Government should set up its own office of public debt

- o Banks and FIs fulfilling well-defined criteria may be allowed to participate in gold markets in India and abroad and deal in gold products.

The recent spurt in foreign exchange in India raised the demand for immediate liberalization of the capital account. Accordingly, in October 2006, RBI announced measures such as doubling of resident individual remittances to $50,000 per year Resident individuals can remit up to $50,000 per year for any current or capital account transaction or a combination of both, as against the earlier limit of $25,000 Foreign exchange earners may retain up to 100% of their earnings in their Exchange Earners' Foreign Currency accounts. Companies, eligible of accessing External Commercial Borrowings (ECBs) can avail an additional amount of $250 million over and above the existing limit of $500 million per year. RBI increased prepayment of ECBs for corporates from $200 million to $300 million without prior approval and eased norms for corporates to set up offices abroad. Overseas investment limit for mutual funds has been raised to $3 billion as against $2 billion. The existing limit of $2 billion in government securities by foreign institutional investors (FIIs) has been enhanced to $3.2 billion. FIIs can rebook a part of forward contracts. It is proposed to allow FIIs to rebook a part of the cancelled forward contracts, provided such contracts are supported by underlying exposure. Importers could book forward contracts for their customs duty component of imports. Besides, forward contracts booked by exporters and importers in excess of 50% of the eligible limit cannot be cancelled. Asian Development Banks can issue guarantees or letter of credit for import of services up to US $1,00,000 for securing a direct contractual liability arising out of a contract between a resident and a non-resident. RBI eliminated the lock-in period for sale proceeds of the immovable property credited to NRO account, provided the amount being remitted to any financial year does not exceed $1 million.

India has achieved considerable feats in two of the

three fields recommended by Tarapore Committee. Inflation declined from 7% in 1997 to under 4% in 2005. RBI has decided to pursue an inflation target. Proportion of NPA has fallen from 13.7% 1997 to 5.2% in 2005. Trade has been largely liberalized with quotas on imports of consumer goods phased out. However, progress has been limited in context of fiscal discipline. Public sector deficit has increased from 7.3% of GDP in 1997-98 to 7.7% of GDP in 2005-06. The ratio of public debt to GDP has increased from under 65% to over 83%. With one important precondition not yet met, immediate move to CAC might be dangerous. Some might argue that, while most of the South-East Asian countries were characterized by prudent fiscal behaviour, contagion affected them equally badly. However, the experience of Argentina, Chile, Uganda and Brazil suggests that fiscal profligacy could indeed lead to a crisis. Moreover, interest rates, particularly the bank deposit rates, the provident fund rate and long-term interest rates are still administered in India. However, it is not immediately possible to give unlimited access to short-term external borrowings and to give unrestricted freedom to domestic residents to convert their domestic bank deposits and idle assets in response to market developments. These might cause domestic financial vulnerability. Further, adopting flexible exchange rate is easier for a developed rather than a developing nation. Moreover, even if developing nations are to abandon undervalued exchange rate, it would be not justified to allow their exchange rate to be pushed up to an uncompetitive level (*Williamson*, 2006). There is perhaps one justification for retaining fixed exchange rates. If some capital reversal is indeed likely, then "with some nominal wage-price inertia it may be optimal not to have a floating exchange rate regime" (*Sen*, 2006). With flexible exchange rate immediate appreciation and current account deficit would incur output and employment costs. Moreover, as free flow of capital dictates the movement in exchange rate there might be additional burden. Williamson (2006) considers a specific case. If India, for example, sought to maintain spending during a world recession through expansionary macroeconomic policies, it might well find that its reserves got run down even without a strong initial effective appreciation. At that point, the danger would be the more traditional one of a run out of the rupee.

Debt repayment capacity of developing nations is not yet credible to the international market (*Williamson,* 2006). Historically, they have been denied credit during financial crises even if they had satisfactory past record of debt repayment. Winning trust in the international market before moving towards CAC is therefore important.

The fact that a country would be exposed to risks while embracing CAC should not rule out the case for CAC in India. Rather, India should fully prepare itself to cope with all the short run danger that might lurk through such move. Analysts have suggested that as the developing countries grow (particularly in terms of per capita income) they can win market trust and capital control might turn out to be ineffective. This however could take time. Europe moved to CAC after almost thirty years after it initiated the process of liberalization and financial integration after the World War II. Thus, whether to go for CAC is not the problem. It is the cautious approach that is vital.

References

Dooley, M.P., (1996): "A Survey of the Literature on Controls on International Capital Transactions", *IMF Staff Papers,* Vol. 43, pp. 639-87.

Dornbusch, R. (1998): "Capital Controls: An Idea Whose Time is Past", in *Should the IMF Pursue Capital-Account Convertibility, Essays in International Finance,* 207, Princeton University.

Eichengreen *et al.* (1999): "Capital Account Liberalization—Theoretical and Practical Aspects", *Occasional Paper* 172, International Monetary Fund. Washington DC.

Fischer, S., (1998): 'Capital Account Liberalization and the Role of the IMF' in *Should the IMF Pursue Capital-Account Convertibility? Essays in International Finance,* 207, Princeton University.

Gilbert, Christopher L., G. Irwin and D. Vines, (2000): "International Financial Architecture, Capital Account Convertibility and Poor Developing Countries", paper presented in an ODI Seminar, "*Capital Account Liberalisation: The Developing Country Perspective*", Overseas Development Institute, London, 21st June.

Giovannini, A., and M. de Melo (1993): "Government Revenue from Financial Repression", *American Economic Review,* Vol. 83, pp. 953-63.

Goldstein, M. (1998): "The Asian Financial Crisis: Causes, Cures, and Systematic Implications Policy Analyses in International Economics", 55, Institute for International Finance, Washington DC.

Griffith-Jones, S., J. Williamson and R. Gottschalk (2005): *Should Capital Controls Have a Place in the Future International Monetary System?*, Institute of Development Studies.

Karunaratne, N.D. (2001): "The Issue of Current Account Convertibility—A Post Currency Crisis Perspective", *Discussion Papers in Economics*, No. 288, May.

McKinnon, R.I. (1973): *Money and Capital in Economic Development*, Washington DC, Brookings Institution.

Methora, R. (1989): Exchange rate variability and convertibility, some methodological issues, *EPW*, March 18, pp. 579-84.

Murty, M.S. (1992): "Forcasting Exchange Rate" in M. Thomas Paul (Ed.), *International Monetary Banking and Trade System and Economic Development* (NIBM, Pune), pp. 221-26.

Narashimham, M. (1994): "Financial Sector Reform: The Unfinished Agenda" in *IEA 76th Conference Volume*, Bombay. pp 1-5.

Razin, A., and E. Sadka (1991): 'Efficient Investment Incentives in the Presence of Capital Flight', *Journal of International Economics*, Vol. 31, pp. 171-81.

Rodrik, D. (1998): "Who Needs Capital-Account Convertibility'? in *Should the IMF Pursue Capital-Account Convertibility, Essays in International Finance*, 207, Princeton University.

Sen, P. (2006): "Case Against Rushing into Full Capital Account Convertibility", *Economic and Political Weekly*, pp. 1853-57, May 13.

Tarapore Committee, *Report of the Committee on Capital Account Convertibility*, Reserve Bank of India, Mumbai.

Williamson, J. (2006): "Why Capital Account Convertibility in India is Premature?", *Economic and Political Weekly*, pp: 1848-1850, May 13.

8

India Towards Capital Account Convertibility

Debesh Bhowmik and Debendra Kumar Das

Abstract

This paper will study the pros and cons of capital account convertibility of Rupee. Simply, the capital account convertibility of Rupee means that Rupee can be converted to dollar or any other key currency/currency baskets for acquisition of capital assets abroad including financial and real assets. The issue of capital account convertibility involves to set in (i) pre-conditions, (ii) future restrictions on capital flows, (iii) macroeconomic policies.

There are certain merits as well as demerits of capital account convertibility. Demerits include some risk factors such as excessive capital flows, greater volatility of exchange rate, which destabilizes macroeconomic stability. It pressurizes external reserve and creates greater risk of external stability. All these factors distort equilibrium BoP and produce excessive imbalance in capital account.

IMF Study showed that the success of capital account convertibility is independent of exchange rate of regimes showing examples of Hong Kong, Germany, Indonesia, Thailand, Malaysia.

But EMS and many countries proved that NEER and REER are dependent on exchange rate where capital is fully mobile. In India, REER and NEER are functions of volume of trade and exchange rate depreciation/appreciation

Our study shows that one percent decrease in NEER has induced to rise in exports by 2.97% and imports by 2.91% per year within the period from 1965-66 to 1990-91 and one percent decrease in REER has induced to increase in exports by 3.19% and imports by 3.25% per year during 1965-66 to 1990-91. But, in the post-reform period during 1991-92 to 2003-04, one percent decrease in NEER has led to increase in exports by 2.08% per year and imports by 2.58% per year. One percent decrease in REER has led to 2.75% increase in exports and 2.57% in imports per year. Also, the volatility of NEER and REER are higher in pre-reform period than the post-reform period (measured by coefficient of variation). To conclude, it can be said that India may succeed to go in for full convertibility of Rupee if she manages capital controls and degree of financial integration in every macroeconomic issues.

I. INTRODUCTION

In the New Economic Policy, Government of India plans to globalize Indian economy through various steps in which Rupee convertibility is one of them. In the mean time trade and current account convertibility have been successfully implemented since 1991. Now, India is proceeding towards capital account convertibility so that full convertibility of Rupee be established in the offing. In this paper, we will endeavour to study the pros and cons of capital account convertibility of Rupee.

II. THE MEANING OF CAPITAL ACCOUNT CONVERTIBILITY

Currency of a country is deemed to be convertible on capital account when the local financial assets can be converted into foreign financial assets and *vice versa*, at market determined exchange rates without government controls, regulations, etc. Simply, capital account convertibility means Rupee can be converted to Dollar or any other key currency/currency baskets for acquisition of capital assets abroad including financial and real assets. Capital account convertibility can globalize Indian capital account because it will integrate Indian capital account and it will integrate Indian economy into world economy in the mobility of capital.

The issue of capital account convertibility is how to attract capital and other productive resources from abroad including official grants, loans, technical assistance, private capital and expertise, etc. The issue involves to set in: (i) preconditions, (ii) future restrictions on capital flows, and (iii) macroeconomic policies with numerous difficulties. It also refers to freedom from exchange controls, taxes and subsidies applicable to transactions in capital account of balance of payments, etc. The merits of capital account convertibility are as follows:

(a) It will benefit individual, bank, corporates, FIIs, etc.
(b) It will boost derivative trading in India.
(c) Capital account convertibility can yield many efficiency gains, e.g., by setting prices right; CAC will facilitate efficient intermediation so that borrowers find lower funding cost and savers attain higher returns. Savers and investors will get to use the world market for risk diversification and vulnerability to their wealth and income to domestic economic stocks.
(d) It will stimulate efficiency specialization and innovation.
(e) It will inspire the confidence of potential foreign investors.
(f) It encourages foreigners to share in technology, management practices and markets in domestic enterprises.
(g) It outweighs the distortions introduced by convertibility limited to current account in taking risk.

The introduction of capital account convertibility can help to attract capital inflows, which depends heavily on whether interest rate after tax, and initial capital investment can be repatriated. This is true for all forms of direct investment flows and portfolio capital flows. There are several factors in fulfilling the effectiveness of convertibility in attracting private capital inflows. These are country's economic and legal environment, macroeconomic stability, investment opportunity elsewhere, quality of infrastructure, human capital and natural resources and political stability, etc. of which the macroeconomic stabilization policy for capital account convertibility requires the following series of measures like (i) inflation rate should be brought under control, (ii) sustainable high growth rate, (iii) lower rate of fiscal deficit, (iv) global competitive interest rate, (v) sustainable high growth rate of exportables, (vi) reliable infrastructure, (vii) world class system of financial apparatus and (viii) clear government policy towards globalization.

The introduction of capital account convertibility shows, at least in theories, several risk factors such as;

(a) Capital account convertibility produces excessive volatility of capital flows.
(b) It ensures greater volatility of exchange rate.
(c) It pressurizes external reserve.
(d) Interest rate creates volatility due to its divergence.
(e) Strong exchange rate pressure destabilizes macroeconomic stability.
(f) It creates greater risk of external stability.
(g) Bankruptcy may be seen in case of weaker bank as an effect of (a) and (b).

All these risk factors distort the equilibrium in the balance of payments creating excessive imbalance in the capital account. The disequilibrium in BoP can be corrected by increasing higher reserve and changing exchange rate in the fixed rate policy and on the other hand, by non-inflationary growth strategy with fluctuating exchange rate in the floating mechanism. At an early stage of convertibility, less developed countries suffer from disequilibrium in BoP due to imbalance of current account which can also induce capital account imbalance subsequently.

An interesting debate arises when IMF-study shows that the success of capital account convertibility is independent of exchange rate regimes. The IMF cited examples of Hong Kong, Germany, Indonesia, Thailand and Malaysia. But, it was shown in ERM that excessive volatility of exchange rate appears due to floating rate than that of fixed rate even when capital is completely mobile. Moreover, interest rate convergence is more prominent in the floating than in the fixed rate which was seen in EMS but not seen in dollar convertible areas. After the breakdown of Bretton Woods, the long-run trend of NEER and REER proved that these are not independent of exchange rate regimes where capital is fully mobile. Even in the application of target zone principle of exchange rate, the convergence criteria and the macroeconomic stability are fulfilled in the ERM and in industrialized countries where freely floating exchange rate is valid rather than the fixed rate, since the target zone is a non-linear compromise between fixed exchange rate and freely floating exchange rate. Now, in case of Indian scenario if the rate of inflows exceeds that of outflows, exchange rate is likely to appreciate to the detriment of export growth. Consequently, RBI intervenes in the market to buy the US Dollar by pumping Rupee resources. Conversely, if Rupee slides significantly, RBI sells the US Dollar at the interventionist rate to push up the exchange rate.

III. RUPEE CONVERTIBILITY, LONG-RUN EXCHANGE RATE MECHANISM AND BALANCE OF PAYMENTS

Traditional literature (*Yeager,* 1976) argues that there was no correlation between exchange rate variability on trade throughout the 19th century. But studies in the mid and late 1980s showed more convincing adverse effect of exchange rate variability on trade. But exchange rate variability in LDCs coupled with developed country's protectionism may have a measurable impact on trade and income (*Methora,* 1989). *V.G. Joshi* (1990) tested the monetary approach to BoP under managed floating in India and estimated exchange market pressure equation for Rupee-Dollar, Rupee-Sterling and Rupee-composite currency rates with quarterly data

(1976-1993). He found that the monetary authorities can determine to achieve various exchange rate targets. Murty (1992) argued BoP (Mundell-Fleming model) is a good fit for forecasting exchange rate under fixed rate but limited to floating rate whereas PPP theory indicates long-run equilibrium exchange rate and is good only for long-term forecasting. And portfolio balance model has not found strong significant about future exchange rates whereas PPP is still a reasonable anchor for long-run exchange rate expectation (*Paul,* 1992). The extreme contention is that exchange rate cannot be forecasted because of unpredicted economic factors and political conditions.

The Rupee convertibility can be well explained with the behaviour of exchange rate variation and its implication of Indian balance of trade and balance of payments even when long-run exchange rate mechanism is applied. Under long-run exchange rate mechanism, one percent depreciation in exchange rate promotes 0.66% increase in export and higher is the elasticity of real effective exchange rate, the higher is the value of exportable (*Rangarajan,* 1991). Also, the declining trend of NEER and REER signifies the increase in growth rate of exports which can promote export competitiveness and stabilizes external value of Rupee (*Kumar and Joseph,* 1994). There are lacunae of this view. The study of Sarkar (1992) revealed that there existed no significant impact between India's BoP and exchange rate whether BoT is measured in terms of Rupee, Dollar and SDR. His regression analysis during 1971-91 confirmed that the depreciation of Rupee has no favourable impact on Dollar value and volume of export and no contractionary effect on the value and volume of import. For better off in export competitiveness in LDCs, depreciation tends to successive depreciation. This view was enriched by R. Sau (1993) who derived a first-order non-linear difference equation for exchange rate estimating quarterly data of US Dollar relative to SDR during 1974-91 and forecasted the value of Dollar up to the first quarter of 1995. The study revealed that the Dollar would be upswing in the offing, which might effect the Indian Rupee ever if made fully convertible to depreciate relative to Dollar.

The above relationship is not unanimously true because

there is no unique relationship between increasing growth of exportable and downward REER. In my regression analysis, it was found that in the pre-reform period from 1965-66 to 1990-91, one percent decrease in NEER induced increase in export by 2.9756% and imports by 2.9166% per year. On the other hand, one percent decrease in REER led to increase in export by 3.192% and imports by 3.2568% per year respectively. But, during the post-reform period from 1991-92 to 2003-04, one percent increase in NEER led to increase in export by 2.08217% and one percent decrease in NEER led to increase in import by 2.5827% per year. The relation between NEER and export is found insignificant. Again, one percent increase in REER led to increase in import by 2.5788% per year and was found insignificant. And, one percent decrease in REER led to 2.7549% increase in export per year and was found significant (Table 1). It is interesting to note that the volatility of NEER and REER affect the behaviours of export and import but the volatility of both the NEER and REER are higher in the pre-reform period than the reform period. For example, the coefficient of variation of NEER is 26.187% in pre-reform period and 12.765% in the post-reform period. Again, the skewness and kurtosis are 1.576 and 6.353 in pre-reform period but 1.2168 and 3.8709 respectively in the post-reform period.

Again, the coefficient of variation of REER is 23.8566% in pre-reform period and 6.2994% in post-reform period. The skewness and kurtosis are 0.837 and 3.4044 in pre-reform and 0.1867 and 3.2072 in the post-reform period respectively. Not only that, the downward trends of NEER and REER were not confirmed in all the periods such as REER showed increasing trend in the post-reform period, i.e. increased at the rate of 1.17% per year from 1991-92 to 2003-04 which was verified by the semi-log linear model. (Table 2).

These may be corrected through proper exchange rate policy with good management technique including significant exchange rate forecasting because, in EMS, fixed rate in the region and floating rate outside the region were applied whereas in NAFTA, Japan, Australia, etc. floating rate was eventually working well. Due to efficient working of convergence criteria, volatility of exchange rate is mild in EU with low macroeconomic fundamentals and without speculative attack whereas there is no convergence criteria in NAFTA, ASEAN or in other countries where capital is mobile but they have been facing speculative attack due to monetary shock and weak macroeconomic fundamentals. Thus, to avoid contagion effects of crisis for opening up of capital, India needs strong current account and manageable short-run financial commitment to go for full convertibility with controlled money supply in freely floating exchange rate along with adjustments in the BoP. Hence, the most important notion is that during the process of financial opening, there should be consistency between exchange rate and monetary policy as predicted in currency crisis model. If crawl rate is less than depreciating shadow floating rate, then speculative attack begins. So, in the policy framework, forcing the space of financial opening steps up speed at which the shadow exchange rate is increasing. Then the nominal exchange rate must depreciate equally fast to ward off speculative attacks and attracts reserves. These would bring depreciating-induced inflation which is inimical to growth. On the other hand, if we resort to monetary expansion to coax growth, it would, apart from exacerbating inflation, increase the shadow exchange rate still further, thereby, diluting the potency of exchange rate management to ward-off currency crisis. On the contrary, in the limited case, there is no need for nominal exchange rate to depreciate as fast as before to keep up with shadow exchange rate. Thus domestic credit can be increased to track growth with little inflation. So, the continued consistency between monetary policy, exchange rate policy and pace of opening will produce sustainable financial openness where Thailand, Philippines, Malaysia, Indonesia and Korea led fairly high financial openness indices while India and Taiwan with low indices escaped the currency crises. This provokes to abandon any pre-commitment towards capital account convertibility (*Rao and Singh,* 1998). More crucially, it is to examine that the effectiveness index of depreciation (measured by NEER/REER) was stronger and favourable for 1966 devaluation during 1967-68 to 1972-73 except in 1966-67 (when BoP on current account balance improved) and it was more effective after 1975-76 onwards for a decade or more (BoP improved). But, it was emphasized that the effectiveness index of depreciation had stepped down by the depreciation of 1991 showing decelerating values of effectiveness index of depreciation. The semi-log linear model states that effectiveness index of depreciation increased at the rate of 0.049% per year during 1965-66 to 1990-91 and decreased 3.918% per year during 1991-92 to 2003-04 respectively.

In another study, I showed that trade elasticities did not produce any comprehensive result on trade balances in our Rupee exchange rate variation with 28 foreign currencies under managed and freely floating exchange rate mechanism during the reform period from 1990-91 to 1991-2000 (*Bhowmik*, 2001).

IV. TARAPORE COMMITTEE AND INDIAN CAPITAL ACCOUNT CONVERTIBILITY

Tarapore Committee has prepared a report on preconditions to pave the way of success of Indian Capital Account Convertibility within 2000 AD. They recommended that India must maintain: (i) inflation rate at 3.5%, (ii) fiscal deficit at 3.5% of GDP (iii) debt service to 20%, and (iv) current account deficit at 1.6% of GDP along with high growth rate of GDP to ensure macroeconomic stability in three phases within 2000 AD. The report also suggested the sequence of measures to (i) reduce NPA to 5% and CRR to 3%, (ii) cut down the growth rate of M3 within 15%, (iii) deregulate interest rate which is to be determined freely in the market, (iv) increase foreign exchange reserves up to at least three months imports, and (v) increase the efficiency of risk management. in banks and non-banks, etc. The Committee endorsed target zone exchange rate within ± 5% around the neutral REER. Also free flow of gold, EDI, NRI investment, corporate and bank investment/borrowing will be allowed. Private and non-banks are needed to expand more. Disinvestment and liberalization are to be continued speedily. The Second Tarapore Committee on capital account convertibility stretched to realize it in three phases ending 2011 strengthening on banking sector reform and fiscal policy.

The preconditions will be fulfilled with a step by step approach slowly but steadily. In evaluating the preconditions the performance of the economy is to be judged analytically with empirical verification. In case of inflation rate India experienced average rates of 8.4% and 9.7% during 1970-80 and 1984-94 and 10.2% and 9.0% and 3.0% in 1995, 1996, and 2000 respectively. Also, average inflation rate is found as 4.46% from 2000-01 to 2005-06. Hence the target rate of 3.5% will surely be unachievable within a very short period. But, it is necessary to acquire price stability to maintain target zone of ± 5.0% around neutral REER as the first condition with exchange rate as the second condition.

Secondly, India's average fiscal deficit during 1992-93 to 1999-2000 was 5.33% of GDP as against 7.0% in 1990-91. Again, the average fiscal deficit during 2000-01 to 2005-06 was 5.1% of GDP. So, it is an Herculean task before the government to achieve 3.5% of GDP without massive cut in subsidies, non-plan expenditure and defence spending, etc. or to increase resource mobilization with a higher rate. It is hopeful to think that the 10th Plan target computed it as 4.0% of GDP. Hence, Tarapore-II banned on any further issue of participatory notes and Lahiri Committee mandated that Foreign Institutional Investors should issue participatory notes.

Thirdly, India could maintain current account deficit of 1.2% of GDP during 1991-99 in her external balance in comparison with the target rate of 1.6% of GDP in 2000 as directed by the Tarapore Committee. During 2000-01 to 2004-05, the average current account deficit as percentage of GDP was found as 0.58% of GDP which is hopeful. Of course, it is not the sufficient policy to stabilize exchange rate which may, on the contrary, ensure current account stability. The Committee emphasized also high rate synonymous with Ninth Plan for other macroeconomic preconditions. India secured 5.71% growth rate of national income during 1991-2000 and also secured 6.35% average growth rate of national income during 2000-01 to 2005-06. Thus Tenth Plan is also permissible to realize the preconditions of capital account convertibility. It is interesting to note that a high growth rate did not necessarily mean a lower current deficit, lower fiscal deficit with stable exchange race in case of India in the last few years.

Fourthly, high debt-GDP and debt-service ratio of India have hindered its growth rate and delayed in financial sector reform. The heavy dose of debt burden is caused due to unending external imbalance leading to wider gap of export and import growth rates in India during long years. This implied a tremendous pressure on debt-GDP ratio that was 41.0% in 1992 and fell to 23.7% in 1998-99 and also implied pressure on debt service ratio which were 8.0% in 1998-99 and 24.3% in 1995-96 in comparison with 35.3% in 1990-91 whereas Tarapore Committee wished to reduce it to 20% in 2000. Now, we are very much hopeful that the external debt as percent of GDP is computed as 19.8% on an average during 2000-01 to 2004-05. This would boost export-oriented growth strategy with strong external sector.

Fifthly, the Committee recommended liberalization and continuation of economic reform that might enhance NRI investment, foreign direct investment and other capital inflows. FDI stood a record level of 14,330 million dollar in 1999 in comparison to 129 million dollar in 1991-92 but in 2005, FDI stood at 7.4 billion dollar which is 0.8% of the global share of FDI. Portfolio investment increased to 4.2 billion dollar in September, 2005 from 1360 million dollar in 1999 and from 4 million dollar in 1991-92 respectively where NRI played insignificant role since 1996-97. Yet, the FII flows reached at level of 339 million dollar in September,2004. These are none the less satisfactory. The achievement of Indian capital market reform is remarkable because 75% of Indian market capitalization is now owned by FII. India has the largest listed companies. BSE sensex stood at 10,370 on 28-2-06, as against 6219 in February, 2000. Also, S&P CNX-500 stood at 2658 on 28-2-06 as against 1557 in April 7, 2000. But Nifty analysis showed a low correlation of-minus 0.0198 between US stock market and Indian S&P in the data of 17 years. The growth of international trade and integration of India's financial market through FII convertibility are the factors accounting for greater correlation between India and the global economy. The front tier of stocks in the NSE saw a rise in this correlation with the US from 0.26 to 0.35 during

2002-05. The second tier of stocks Nifty Junior had also seen correlation with the US rise from 0.17 to 0.26. (*Economic Survey,* 2005-06). Moreover, the competitiveness of India in the world capital market is improving slowly. The index of internationalization of India is 41. Therefore, the derivative trading in India is needed for quick capital market reform. This will require speedy banking and financial sector reform with international standard.

Sixthly, the Committee suggested to cut down CRR to 3%, NPA to 5% and growth rate of M3 to 15% within 2000 AD.. The Indian Banking scenario showed that gross NPA stood at 16.12 and net NPA stood at 8.2% in 1998, and now NPA to gross advance is reached at 5.2% in March 2005, but 14 out of 42 foreign banks had no NPA, 20 banks had NPA below 10% and 6 had NPA above 10% (*RBI,* 1999).The cause of high NPA in India are lacunae in credit recovery, weak in loan appraisal, sickness of banks, labour problem, etc. Besides, the profitability is lower in Indian banks than the foreign banks. Recently, RB1 cut CRR to 5%, bank rate to 6% and repo rate to 6.5% in February, 2006. Will these policies keep up the M3 growth rate at 15%? It is observed that the average growth rate of during 2000-01 to 2005-06 was found as 15.15%. So, it is hopeful to be a green signal towards capital account convertibility within a very short period. It requires speedy reform in banking sector in the areas of credit, deposit, profitability and management, etc.

Seventhly, Indian interest rate is not completely deregulated, which was emphasized by the Tarapore Committee. The policy will make Indian interest rate close to international level for increasing competitiveness. Recently, the real interest rate cut down from 8.8% (1986-91) to 5.7% (2000-05) to come closer to international level.

If India follows the policies of globalization and liberalization to allow target zone, then the exchange rate becomes less volatile at the expense of raising interest rate volatility. Then there arises a dilemma of maintaining convergence criteria in LDC to reduce both the volatility of exchange rate and interest rate. We know that the exchange rate is completely random and there is a strong significant relationship between exchange rate and interest rate differentials. It is not independent of international BoP. Thus it may be written that exchange rate to be a function of national price level, interest rate and international balance of payments.

Lastly, Indian foreign exchange reserves are mounting from 15068 million dollar in 1993-94 to 35,061 million dollar in 2000, and finally reached to 140 billion Dollar in February 2006 which is enough for facing random exogenous shocks. It is not completely independent of exchange rate behaviour of home or abroad. Maintaining external balance is crucial to increase these reserves. We know that convertibility of a currency of a nation may or may not stimulate the volume of foreign exchange reserve and high powered money. An upward movement of volume of forex reserves occurs due to several reasons such as (i) an increase in external debt from international institutions and foreign countries, etc., (ii) an inflow of foreign currencies as aid, gifts, donations and NRI deposits, etc., (iii) an increase in portfolios from foreign countries, and (iv) an increase in FDI inflows due to liberalization as a result of positive BoT and BoP from which foreign currencies may enhance due to rising trend of export growth. The items (i) and (ii) can meet up demands for international liquidity whereas they would be burdened to the national economy. In this case the high reserves do not necessarily mean the efficient management of currency (*Black*, 1993). Also, a drain of convertible currencies would occur in the long-run. The items (iii) and (iv) can yield positive result for convertibility. If there are good management of downward REER, and upward export elasticities in case of (iv), the increase of foreign currencies brings stimulating effect on national income. On the contrary, a low foreign exchange reserve with efficient management of currency maintaining internal stability of the economy, can yield a better result from convertibility. Moreover, the random shocks into the economy due to inflation would be higher in (i) and (ii) than in (iii) and (iv).

Now, it is important and an Herculean task to fix neutral REER with band ± 5.0% because India faced excessive volatility of exchange rate. Although volatility is lower in the reform period than the pre-reform period in respect of coefficient of variation of both NEER and REER respectively. Again, if REER is to be the indicator then RBI should publish weekly data of REER. The weights and base year to calculate REER are crucial to follow freely floating exchange rate mechanism. Care should be taken to such measures. Besides, random walk hypothesis of REER in India should not be the final goal; the time series instability of real exchange rate and market volatility measured by conditional variances follow a persistent non-linear behaviour attended with oscillations due to complex characteristic roots should be an added explanation.

V. CONCLUDING REMARKS

Implementation of full convertibility of Rupee is not the new concept in Indian economy in the sense of globalization. The Rupee was also fully convertible to Pound-Sterling under the British Rule in which the management of a currency was rather very weak because the gold standard and the circulation of gold currency were not applied. Thus, the Rupee convertibility was deferred, delegalized, delocalized and therefore a devitalized kind of convertibility. Really, it was not an act of convertibility, but rather it was a moratorium which was a negation of convertibility in practice (*Ambedkar*, 1947, *Bhowmik*, 1994). The Indian currency system then produced "a drain" of convertible Pound-Sterling from India to UK as a result of latter's imperialism. With the same reason, we can argue that the recent dollar convertible Rupee may lead to drain of dollar to U.S.A., which will ultimately strengthen U.S. imperialism in the offing.

Irrespective of that, the success of full convertibility of Rupee, depends on the degree of achievement on monetary integration and financial integration in the global market and also depends on how far Indian currency system can link with international monetary system Moreover, volatility of interest and exchange rate are the random disturbing factors by which Indian capital market has been distorted regularly. The deregulation of financial sectors should be well managed in such a way so that the process of market integration along with European and American market generate efficient

TABLE I

Pre-reform period (1965-66 to 1990-91)	Post-reform period (1991-92 to 2004-05)
Log (export) =22.4392 - 2.9756 log NEER) (- 8.7977)* (14.220)* R^2=0.763, DW=0.35, F=77.40*	log (export) =2.1968 + 2.08217 log (NEER) (0.1 329)* (0.4601)* R^2=0.018, DW=2.33, F=0.216
Log (export) =23.6147 - 3.9120 log (REER) (16.276)* (-10.370)* R^2=0.817, DW=0.853, F=107.721*	log (export) =21.1708 - 2.7549 log (REER) (0.589) (-0.3165) R^2=0.009, DW=2.34, F=0.1002
Log (import) =22.517 - 2.9166 log (NEER) (10.262)* (-6.2017)* R^2=0.615, DW=0.261, F=38.46	log (import) =19.9137 - 2.5827 log (NEER) (19.252)* (-9.1195)* R^2=0.883, DW=1.97, F=83.165*
Log (import) =24.2732 - 3.2568 log (REER) (12 254)* (-7.756)* R^2=0.714, DW=0.639, F=60.162*	log (import) =-0.1609 + 2.5788 log (REER) (-0.0282) (1.866)* R^2=0.2405, DW=0.571, F=3.483*

Source: *EPW*, Various Issues, India Development Report, 1997, 1999-00, 2004-05.
*=significant at least 10% level.

mechanism of currency management in India (*Crawford*, 1993). Moreover, Indian policy-makers should be aware about the pace of higher degree of liberalization in times of signing MIGA or MAI to boost capital market in order to fight against contagious effects of currency crises and also to avoid macroeconomic failures. Above all, political decision on the part of the government is vital for complete implementation of Rupee convertibility. Lastly, if Indian government can manage to control large real exchange rate appreciation, declining exports and foreign exchange reserves, large decline in industrial production, sharp increase in the ratio of M2 to reserve and weak macroeconomic fundamentals which were observed in 19 countries of East Asia, Europe, Latin America and West Africa during 1970-95, then India may succeed to go in for full convertibility of Rupee if she manages capital control and degree of financial integration in every

TABLE 2

Pre-reform period (1965-66 to 1990-91)	*Post-reform period (1991-92 to 2004-05)*
Log (export) =7.1764 + 0.1035t (109.53)* (24.396)* R^2= 0.96	log (export) = 10.4093 - 0.08738t (9.44)* (-0.629) R^2=0.034
Log (import) =7.4293 + 0.11091t (75.65)* (17.44)* R^2= 0.926	log (import) =9.967 + 0.0740t (99.808)* (5.8852)* R^2=0.758
Log (NEER) =5.0277 - 0.02726t (108.229)* (-9.065)* R^2=0.77	log (NEER) =3.8425 - 0.0274t (112.592)* (-6.38)* R^2=0.787
Log (REER) =5.0817 - 0.02738t (134.058)* (-11.156)*. R^2=0.838	log (REER) =4.046 + 0.0117t (151.89)* (3.49)* R^2=0.52
For NEER Co-efficient of variation=26.187% Skewness=1.576 Kurtosis=6.353	For NEER Co-efficient of variation=12.765% Skewness=1.2168 Kurtosis=3.8709
For REER Co-efficient of variation=23.856% Skewness=0.837 Kurtosis=3.4044	For REER Co-efficient of variation=6.2994% Skewness=0.1867 Kurtosis=3.2072
Log (EID)=0.05758 + 0.00049t (0.208) (-1.58) R^2=0.0018	log (EID) =-0.2045 - 0.03918t (-10.15)* (-15.43)* R^2=0.955

EID=NEER/REER=Effectiveness Index of depreciation.
*=Significant at least 10% level.
Source: *EPW, Various Issues, India Development Report*, 1997, 1999-00, 2004-05.

macroeconomic issues although benefits of capital account liberalization in terms of higher growth and lower volatility seem to be most evident for the industrial economies. Even, the government can also observe the variables that have the best track record in anticipated crises in the signal approach which include output, exports, deviations of the real exchange rate from trend, equity prices, ratio of broad money to gross international reserves and other supporting indicators like imports, the differential between foreign and domestic real deposit interest rates, the ratio of lending to deposit interest rates, and bank deposit. (*Colaco Francis*, 1997).

References

Aghevli, B.B. and P.J. Monteil (1996): "Exchange Rate Policies in Developing Countries" in Frankel J.A. and M. Goldstein. (Eds.), *Functioning of the International Monetary System*, Vol. 2, (IMF), pp. 612-43.

Ambedkar, B.R. (1947): *History of Indian Currency and Banking*, Vol. I. (Bombay).

Bhowmik, Debesh (2002): *Essays on International Money*, Deep and Deep Publications, New Delhi.

———1989): "Proposal for a New World Monetary Order," *Economic Studies*, Vol. 27, No. 4, pp. 25-31.

———(1994): "A Profile of Dr. B.R. Ambedkar's View on the Concept of Convertibility of Rupee," *IEA 76th Conference Volume*, Bombay, pp. 14-16.

———(1996): "Convertibility, Exchange Rate Behaviour and India's Trade during 1960-61 to 1992-93: An Analysis," *Southern Economist*, March 15, pp. 11-14.

———(1999): "Exchange Rate Behaviour in India during 1968-97", *IEA Conference Volume*, Amritsar, pp. 352-62.

———(2001): "Economic Reforms, India's Trade and Rupee Depreciation", *Southern Economist*, November 1, pp. 7-9.

Black, S.W. (1993): "Management of International Liquidity in Developing Countries," *ADB 3rd International Seminar Paper*, New Delhi.

Colaco Francis, X. (1997): East Asian Currency Crises, Rougue Traders, Fundamentals, Contagion, *EPW*, 6 December, pp. 3129-38.

Crawford. M. (1993): *One Money for Europe?*, Macmillan.

Economic Times (1997): "The Road to Convertibility", (Tarapore Committee Report), 4-6-1997.

EPW Research Foundation (1996): *Mapping a Risky Path: Capital Account Convertibility Report*, June 7, pp. 1300-03.

Joshi, V.G. (1990): "Monetary Approach to BOP and Exchange Rate: Empirical Evidence Relating Specially to India," *Artha Vijnana*, September-December, Vol. 32, Nos. 3, 4, pp. 270-80.

Kamaiah, B., P. Nandakumar, H.K. Pradhan (1992): "On Random Walk Characteristics of Exchange Rates, Some Further Evidence," in M.Thomas Paul (Ed.), *International Monetary, Banking and Trade System and Economic Development*, NIBM, Pune, pp. 187-200.

Kose, M.A., E. Prasad (2004): "Liberalising Capital", *Finance and Development*, September 2004, pp. 50-51.

Kumar, R., M. Joseph (1994): "External Value of Rupee," *IEA 76th Conference Volume*, Bombay, pp. 4-8.

Methora, R. (1989): "Exchange Rate Variability and Convertibility, Some Methodological Issues," *EPW*, March 18, pp. 579-84.

Murty, M.S. (1992): "Forcasting Exchange Rate" in M. Thomas Paul (Ed.), *op. cit.*, pp. 221-26.

Narashimham, M. (1994): "Financial Sector Reform: The Unfinished Agenda," *IEA 76th Conferenc Volume*, Bombay, pp. 1-5.

Pillai, G.K. (1994): "Determinants of Exchange Rate: Theories and Evidence", *IEA 76th Conference Volume*, Bombay, pp. 33-37.

Rangarajan, C. (1991): "The Exchange Rate System, Some Key Issues", *IEJ*, Vol. 36, No. 3, pp. 14-27.

Rao, M.J.M. and B. Singh (1998): "Optimising the Pace of Capital Account Convertibility", *EPW*, May 23, pp. 1247-54.

Reddy, Y.V. (2004): "Capital Account Convertibility," Speech delivered in Bank of England on 25-6-2004.

Sarkar, P. (1992): "Rupee Depreciation and India's External Trade and Payments Since 1991", *EPW*, Jan. 13-20, pp. 1259-66.

Sau, R. (1993): "Exchange Rate Dynamics—A Case of Dollar", *EPW*, June 26, pp. 1394-95.

Seshadri, R.K. (1993): *From Crisis to Convertibility*, Orient Longman, Calcutta.

Varghese, W. (1992): "Forecasting Exchange Rate," in M. Thomas Paul (Ed.) *op. cit.*, pp. 169-86.

Yeager, L.B. (1976): *International Monetary Relation: Theory, History and Policy*, New York, Harper and Row.

9

Capital Account Convertibility in India: Issues and Challenges

SANKHANATH BANDYOPADHYAY

ABSTRACT

Regarding the issue of Capital Account Convertibility (CAC), there are a number of theoretical benefits and associated costs of CAC that have been discussed and empirically tested by several academicians. The important point to note is that whether a country is in a position to take advantage of CAC by maximizing (or at least maintaining) the net benefit through CAC. A pessimistic attitude may point to the East-Asian crisis. The countries experienced associated stock market and real estate boom and bullish financial market before severe crisis. Whether India is ready to digest the impact of CAC over the long-run is a vital question. Though India is in a much favorable position with strong macroeconomic fundamentals, sound financial market, huge FOREX reserves, and low external debt, still some important anomalies are present which needs to be taken care of before approaching towards full CAC. The timing and sequencing should be carefully judged as the macroeconomic conditions differ among countries and the benefits of CAC are largely country specific.

This paper is distributed over three sections. In the first section, some of the most important factors helping India to maintain surplus in the BOP are identified and to what extent they are reliable in order to maintain the external viability of the Indian economy is also tried to be assessed, since if these sources are stable and reliable, then a strong argument can be made for introducing CAC in India and vice versa. Some feasible policy prescriptions are also discussed. In the second section, some specific issues related to the monetary and fiscal policies and corporate debt market, which are sensitive to the aspect of full Capital Account Convertibility (CAC), are discussed. The last section is for conclusion and policy prescription.

INTRODUCTION

Regarding the issue of Capital Account Convertibility (CAC), there are a number of theoretical benefits and associated costs of CAC that have been discussed and empirically tested by several academicians. The important point to note is that whether a country is in a position to take advantage of CAC by maximizing (or at least maintaining) the net benefit through CAC. A pessimistic attitude may point to the East-Asian crisis; the countries experienced associated stock market and real estate boom and bullish financial market before severe crisis. Whether India is ready to digest the impact of CAC over the long-run is a vital question. Suppose a country will be in a sustainable growth path after twenty years. But if severe crisis starts to occur within five years, the country even may not reach the target and the short-run cost may be severe. Given the potential risk factors associated with CAC, an important question is 'is it necessary to introduce full capital account convertibility in India?'

Contrary to the above argument, there are a number of theoretical benefits associated with CAC (which supports the argument why should countries pursue for CAC) which are as follows (*Jadav*, 2003):

- Greater financial efficiency, specialization and innovation by exposing the financial sector to global competition.
- Developing countries need external capital to sustain an excess of investment over domestic

saving and an open capital account could attract larger foreign capital.

- By offering the opportunity of using the world market to diversify portfolios, an open capital account permits both savers and investors to protect the real value of their assets through risk reduction, etc.

Without going into details of the potential benefits of CAC, an important question may be asked: How can we be sure that a country has already possessed the necessary reforms and preconditions to reap all the benefits of CAC? Given the risks associated with the CAC greater macroeconomic instability might arise due to volatility of short-term capital movements and the risks of larger capital outflows) is a country able to pre-empt any potential shock/s once it starts?

Another issue is that how can one understand that the speed and sequencing of necessary reforms in order to perceive the benefits of CAC is perfect for a country so that she can introduce the full CAC? Evidences of the emerging economies (e.g. Thailand, Malaysia) have shown that immediately after opening up their capital account they have enjoyed capital inflows, but ultimately they have faced crises. Is there any guarantee that this would not happen to India also? In my mind, however two counterbalancing arguments are at present; one is 'no risk no gain' (so that one has to decide whether she is a risk averse or a risk lover person) and the other is the factor for which some of these countries faced crisis, are not our headache. (For e.g. there is no asset mismatches due to short-term borrowing and long-term investments, lower external debt, huge FOREX Reserves, etc.). However, this does not mean that there are no anomalies present in our economy sensitive to full CAC (which may be under control of other economies).

It is widely contended that costs outweigh the benefits when the sequencing of liberalization becomes faulty and therefore, it is the attainment of preconditions that should determine the sequencing of liberalization. However, significant ambiguity exists in the empirical studies regarding the relationship between economic growth and CAC itself (*Arteta and others*, 2001). Therefore how can one be sure that even after pursuing full CAC a country would be able to realize significant growth?

However, there are some favorable aspects of the Indian economy which are given below:

- India has achieved a strong economic growth relative to many developed markets. The rate of growth is increasing at faster rate than many other economies.
- India has a more than sufficient FOREX reserves to cover more than 12 months' import, while the benchmark is to cover 3 months' import cover.
- India has a much lower stock of external debt.
- India has lower correlations with the international equities, which improves a portfolio's overall risk-return profile, even if asset specific risk is higher.
- It must also be noted that India's earnings growth rate and return on equity are also one of the highest among other emerging markets and the rest of the world. The return in India is as high as U.S. (0.04 percentage on average) with a moderate volatility of 1.89 percent.

The intra-day volatility (*Raju and others*, 2004) of the stock market in India is much less compared to the stock market of most of the emerging economies.

SECTION I

The rate of growth of imports exceeds the rate of growth of exports in merchandise trade. (Table 1)

The current account surplus is due to surplus in the invisible trade in which service is dominating. (Table 2)

In this category private transfers is the dominating source of all the categories. In some of the years the net inflows in this category is even higher than the overall inflows in the invisibles' category. This implies that private transfers has compensated the net outflows in the other

TABLE I

Value of Exports and Imports of Goods, 1994-95 to April 2, 2005

(US $mn.)

Year	*Exports*	*Imports*	*Trade Balance*	*Rate of change of Exports*	*Rate of change of Imports*
1994-95	26330	28654	-2324	18.4	22.9
1995-96	31797	36678	-4881	5.3	28
1996-97	33470	39133	-5663	4.6	6.7
1997-98	35006	41484	-6478	-5.1	6.0
1998-99	33218	42389	-9171	10.8	2.2
2000-01	36822	49671	-12849	21	17.2
2001-02	44560	50536	-5976	-1.6	1.7
2002-03	52719	61412	-8693	20.3	19.4
2003-04	63843	78149	-14306	21.1	27.3
2004-05	53499	73652	-20153	23.4	33.6

Source: Economic Survey, Government of India, (2005-06).

categories and largely responsible in reducing the overall current account deficit. From Table 2, it can be noted that software services and private transfers are the predominant sources of the foreign exchange inflows in the current account.

The share of the worker remittances in the current account is the most significant among all the other forms of external flows. According to Poonam Gupta, the volatility of remittances is even less than the NRI deposits and portfolio flows (*Gupta*, 2005). The investment decision by the portfolio investors is mainly decided by the objective of maximizing return subject to a given risk. In general, people are risk-averse, so in any situation, which increases risk, portfolio investors are reluctant in investment. On the other hand, remittances are not driven by the investment motive. Remittance are mostly influenced by altruism. Remittances are likely to increase when their family is in distress.

Thus the important factors which broadly help to maintain surplus in the current account are—

TABLE 2

India's Current Account (1993-2005)

Current Account	*93-94*	*94-95*	*95-96*	*96-97*	*97-98*	*98-99*	*99-00*	*00-01*	*01-02*	*02-03*	*03-04*	*04-05*
Merchandise (net)	-4056	-9049	-11359	-14815	-15507	-13246	-17841	-12460	-11574	-10690	-13718	-33702
Invisibles (net) (a+b+c)	2897	5680	5447	10196	10008	9208	13143	9794	14974	17035	27801	31232
(a) Services (net)	534	602	-200	726	1319	2165	4064	1692	3324	3643	10144	15426
Travel (net)	1725	1547	1544	2020	1477	1250	897	693	123	-29	1435	1417
Transportation (net)	-332	-167	-158	-441	-686	-755	-703	-1512	-1306	-736	879	114
Insurance (net)	-72	-29	36	64	57	112	109	47	8	19	56	148
G.n.i.e. (net)	-123	-155	-205	-106	116	272	312	332	235	65	28	-10
Miscellaneous (net)	-664	-594	-1417	-811	355	1286	3449	2132	4264	4324	7746	13727
(b) Transfer (net)	5633	8509	8852	12777	12209	10587	12638	13106	15856	16838	22162	20785
Official (net)	369	416	345	410	379	307	382	252	458	451	554	260
Private (net)	5264	8093	8507	12367	11830	10280	12256	12854	15398	16387	21608	20525
(c) Income (net)	-3270	-3431	-3205	-3307	-3520	-3544	-3559	-5004	-4206	-3446	-4505	-4979
Total Current Account												

Source: Reserve Bank of India: Handbook of Statistics on Indian Economiy.

- Software services
- Private transfers
- Worker remittances

It seems that India needs to diversify the export sector further. The driving forces behind the current account surpluses are rather limited. Despite of being reliable sources for a long time, we cannot rely exclusively on the private transfers (including NRI deposits) alone, as it depends on standard risk and return factors, so that lack of confidence on the part of the investors may be a hindrance to FOREX inflows.

Foreign institutional investment (FII) is another important factor injecting significant FOREX reserves in the Indian economy.

With respect to this some important factors needs to be addressed, as pointed out by Global Development Finance Report, 2006, which are as follows:

FIIs formed nearly 70 percent of foreign investment (FDI plus net portfolio equity flows) in India, whereas in China and Brazil the percentage was 26 and 30 percent respectively.

During January-December 2005, India's current account deficit was $13 billion. If this has not been financed by the huge surplus in capital account, India's overall BoP would have been in deficit. Moreover, the share of FII has been significant in this surplus. Since 2002-03, non-debt creating foreign investment (net) has been performing a major role in creating current account surplus, particularly FII inflows. During 2005, robust FII inflows were more than eleven times higher than such inflows during April-September 2004 (*Economic Survey*, 2005-06)

As per the MSCI index, India is the ninth best performing market in the global emerging markets. The Boston-based emerging market Portfolio research rates India as the third biggest recipient of FII inflows in Asia after Taiwan and Korea. One advantage of FII is that it is a non-debt creating inflows, so that it can finance any deficit without creating any external liabilities/debt. However, given that it is more destabilizing and does not have any employment generation as well as technology spillover effects like FDI, then liberalization policies should be more focused towards FDI rather then FII.

Related to · FII, another problem is regarding the Participatory Notes (PNs). Until August 2004, investment through PNs in India constituted almost 29 percent of the aggregate FIIs and 47 percent in August 2005. The major problem is that the identity of the investor is not disclosed. There is substantial investment through this source, which apparently seems to be beneficial for mitigating the BOP deficit by injecting FOREX reserves, but the riskiness is also growing due to substantial investments through unregulated and unregistered entities. The Tarapore Committee has pointed to this problem, and suggested that FIIs should be prohibited from investing fresh money raised through PNs and existing PN-holders may be provided an exit route and phased out completely within one year. Now, given that significant FII investment is occurring through this source; prohibition of this may pre-empt a significant proportion of FOREX reserves in India, and here lies the strength of the argument that exclusive reliance on FII as a source of FOREX reserves may be a danger.

Regarding Foreign Investment, the liberalization policy should be biased towards Foreign Direct Investment (FDI) rather than Foreign Institutional Investment (FII) in India, in as much as empirical studies of the effects of FDI have reached more definitive conclusions than those on purely financial flows. The relation between growth and FDI is more prominent than that of between growth and portfolio capital flows. Regarding the market size, it is sometimes argued that India fails to utilize her potential market by creating unnecessary high tariff barriers. The ranking of the Indian economy is also much impressive regarding her expected growth in the market size given her highly educated workforce, management talent, cultural affinity, relatively lower cost of labour, etc.

SECTION II

Favorable Factors

The External debt in India is mostly long-term rather than short-term. Moreover, the country has a more than sufficient stock of FOREX Reserves (almost able to cover more than 12 months' import). One of the reasons of the crises in emerging economies is that these economies held external debt of short-term maturities, while they have invested the external borrowings in long-term investments resulting in significant mismatch between the maturity of liabilities and assets.

Government debt is mostly held in local currency; therefore the fear of 'hard debt'/currency mismatches is limited.

The *External debt* is only 21 percent of GDP and the government debt is mostly internal in nature, i.e. held by primarily domestic residents, which reduces the external vulnerabilities.

Unfavorable Factors

Table 3 compares the Macroeconomic and Financial Indicators for India with the similarly rated as well as lower rated developing countries. From Table 3, it can be seen that General Government Debt as a percentage of GDP is much higher compared to similarly rated countries. (85.7 for India as against 61.2 percent compared to similarly rated countries).

The General Government Debt to revenue ratio which is rather a better measure of debt sustainability than the General Government debt of GDP-ratio is much higher (430 percent) compared to similarly rated as well as lower rated countries. (289 and 372 percent respectively).

Compared to the countries that faced financial crises, India's Debt/Revenues is much higher. Moreover, the Revenue/GDP is also much less compared to these countries. The only comfort is that the Revenue/GDP of India is much stable compared to other countries. But, the revenue does not show any increasing tendency over time; therefore, there is still much discomfort regarding a more sustainable debt path in future.

The General government Interest Payments as a percentage of revenue is almost 14 percent higher than that of the similarly rated as well as lower rated countries. (34 percent in India vis-à-vis 20 and 21 percent respectively). Moreover, average interest payments relative to revenue are significant higher than most countries that have experienced crises.

TABLE 3

Indicator	*India*	*Similarly Rated Sovereigns*	*Low-Rated Sovereigns*
Central government financial balance/GDP	-11.6	-3.9	-4.5
Central government revenues/GDP	19.8	21.9	26.0
Central government debt/GDP	85.7	61.2	89.8
Central government debt/ Central government revenues	430.0	289.0	372.0
Central government interest payments Central government revenue	34.0	20.0	21.0
Central government currency and foreign currency indexed debt/ Central government debt	7.8	63.5	72.2
Current account balance/GDP	0.4	-2.3	-3.3

Monetary Implications

The rising FOREX reserves in Indian economy at present is well beyond the security concern, rather it poses a challenge to the RBI of managing such a hefty ever-increasing reserves. Increasing FOREX reserves means that the RBI has to purchase officially FOREX reserves in exchange of domestic currency, which increases the domestic money supply in the economy. There is a traditional theoretical fear that this increase in money supply in domestic economy put additional purchasing power in the hands of the domestic residents, which may lead to a demand-pull inflation. Therefore, the onus of maintaining the price stability lies with RBI. In order to keep the domestic money supply intact, and hence to check potential demand-pull inflation, the RBI is selling securities in the open market in order to curb the additional liquidity. Excess and continuous sell of securities increases the domestic rate of interest by lowering security prices, which attracts more foreign capitals. This in turn, put an upward pressure on domestic exchange rate and causes rupee to appreciate.[1] To what extent this would affect domestic export-competitiveness is a matter of concern. However, more important reason for not allowing rupee to appreciate much is to maintain parity with the other Asian competitors who are pegging their exchange rates in order to maintain global export competitiveness.

Let us consider the following:

$R = ep^*/p$

where,

R: Real Exchange Rate

e: Nominal Exchange Rate

P*: Foreign Price Index

P: Domestic Price Index

Taking log in both sides,

$\ln R = \ln e + \ln p^* - \ln p$

$dR/R = de/e + (dp^*/p^* - dp/p)$

Where the above equation shows that the change in the real exchange rate equals the change in the nominal exchange rate plus the difference between the rate of inflation between the foreign and domestic economy.

Let us consider the following cases:

Case I

If $dp^*/p^* = dp/p$ then $dR/R = de/e$, in this case the change in the real exchange rate equals the change in the nominal exchange rate.[3]

Case II

If $dp^*/p^* < dp/p$ then the change in the real exchange rate depends on the relative changes in the nominal exchange rate *vis-à-vis* the change in the bracketed term.

Case III

$dp^*/p^* > dp/p$ then the change in the real exchange rate depends on the relative changes in the nominal exchange rate vis-à-vis the change in the bracketed term.

For simplicity, we can think of the real exchange rate (R) as the 'relative price of import'. A decline in the real exchange rate implies favorable terms of trade, i.e. importables become cheaper. However, a continuous and significant decline in the real exchange rate means a loss of export-competitiveness for the domestic economy in the international market.

According to the RBI Annual Report, rupee appreciated by 4.4 percent against the Euro, 5.5 percent against the pound sterling and 7.3 percent against the Japanese yen in 2005-06 (March). This means the 'e' in the equation is declining.[2] Again, rate of inflation in India is higher relative to the major advanced economies as well as than China, Korea, South Africa, Mexico, Israel and Malaysia among the emerging economies. This clearly shows that the real exchange rate of the Indian economy is declining; i.e. India is loosing her export-competitiveness in the international market. Though one advantage of exchange rate appreciation is that importable used as inputs in exportable become cheaper which helps Indian exporters in their cost-competitiveness. Nevertheless, the potential threat of losing market also cannot be ignored.

There is a sharp increase of the asset prices in 2005-06. International as well as domestic gold prices have risen sharply. The rise in asset prices, particularly gold, is partly due to the fact that people like to hold gold in an atmosphere of inflation. Therefore, there is a trap; increase in inflation results in further inflation by increasing the demand for gold and its price.

There are some potential adverse consequences of continuous sterilization policy followed by RBI, which are as follows:

- The ability of RBI to sterilize the money supply is under suspicion, given that there must be an upper limit to the government securities in the portfolio of the RBI.

- Continuous and large stock of sterilization through government as well as other forms of interest-bearing instruments increases the liabilities of RBI.
- Recourse to non-market instruments in order to manage the excess liquidity may lead to serious financial sector imbalances.
- As pointed out by the former RBI Governor, Dr. Y.V. Reddy, large holdings of the risk-free financial assets by commercial banks would be a costly affair in the future as long as the future interest risks are considered. The efficiency of the commercial banks may be undermined with respect to the risk management strategies,. in the face of an increasing supply of risk-free assets like government bonds.
- The development of a domestic private bond market might be affected as private sector issuance might be crowded out in the face of a large amount of risk-free public bonds.

The monetary policy problem is becoming severe. On the one hand, continuous sterilization is becoming a costly affair, (particularly given that the stock of government securities is not unlimited and it declines as sterilization continues). Again, the policy of sterilization cannot be given up in the face of higher inflation in India compared to the advanced as well as some of the emerging economies, as low inflation and export competitiveness are important preconditions for full CAC.

Anomalies in Corporate Debt Market

- The Indian corporate markets lack high quality paper, and hence are subject to non-repayment of coupon and principal, which is detrimental to the development of the market. International investments consequent upon full CAC may result significant capital flight if the economic agents face such low quality papers.

- The secondary market for Corporate Debt is much less liquid than is required. One major reason of this is lack of sufficient high quality paper.
- In India, long-term investments like Insurance and Pension funds are rather limited, and are dominated by mutual fund investment, which is largely one-sided, i.e. if money starts flow in it would be in large quantities and if starts going out, the flight will be huge and quick.
- The information related to bond market is neither sufficient nor timely. Without a comprehensive database and transparency, liquidity and investments will be less and sudden shock may not be mitigated.
- The interest rate structure is also very skewed.

CONCLUDING REMARKS

Regarding the issue of Capital Account Convertibility (CAC), there are a number of theoretical benefits and associated costs of CAC that have been discussed and empirically tested by several academicians. The important point to note is that whether a country is in a position to take advantage of CAC by maximizing (or at least maintaining) the net benefit through CAC. A pessimistic attitude may point to the East-Asian crisis: The countries experienced associated stock market and real estate boom and bullish financial market before severe crisis. Whether India is ready to digest the impact of CAC over the long-run is a vital question. Though India is in a much favorable position with strong macroeconomic fundamentals, sound financial market, huge FOREX reserves, and low external debt, still some important anomalies are present which needs to be taken care of before approaching towards full CAC. The timing and sequencing should be carefully judged as the macroeconomic conditions differ among countries and the benefits of CAC are largely country specific.

The post reform period has witnessed that export of goods have risen gradually over the years. But, imports have grown much faster than exports. Therefore, the balance of trade (BoT) deficit continues even after a decade of economic reforms. Though merchandise export grows, there is still need to diversify the export basket.

The net export in the invisible trade is robust, particularly in travel and software services. The growth of the software services is almost 50-60 percent after the post-reform period. The Information and Communication Technology (ICT) have shown remarkable growth. Two factors are important for this growth—

- Growing international demand for ICT services, particularly from US.
- Abundance of human capital in software skills in India.

This sector is contributing almost ten percent of India's exports. Greater incentives can be provided to servicing related to medical transcriptions, content development and pharmaceutical industries. Recent researches have shown that India is the most lucrative destination for Knowledge Process Outsourcing (KPO). In fact, the growth potential in the KPO sector is expected to outpace the BPO. The advantages are cost effectiveness with high-quality manpower, proficiency in English. India's prospect is much better with respect to both current and expected growth in the market size, particularly in software and electronics, travel and tourism, telecommunication and transport industry.

More negotiations on Regional Trading Agreements (RTAs), especially with SAARC countries, particularly with Bangladesh, Bhutan, Sri Lanka, Thailand, and MERCOSUR are more desirable. While maintaining the current trading patterns with the developed countries and gradual shifting through RTAs with the developing economies, India can improve her position in merchandise trade. There are many LDCs who produce necessary industrial intermediate inputs, which are often used by India. Most of these countries are not a direct competitor of India in the international market. Therefore, greater benefit can be realized through RTA.

Though FII has been a reliable source of FOREX

inflows for a long time, higher return and lower risk elsewhere may cause to pull it back from the Indian economy. The only comfort is that we have more than sufficient level of FOREX reserves, so that it can be expected that the country is able to absorb at least any temporary shock. But, can India be treated as a safe haven like the U.S. who still attracts massive financial investment in her capital despite her record level of current account deficit? We should give a careful thought to this factor, keeping in mind that despite maintaining necessary reforms as well as sound macroeconomic policies a country may be in trouble due to greater contagion effect in one or a set of economies in todays' ever increasing financial integration and globalization.

Regarding Foreign Investment, the liberalization policy should be biased towards Foreign Direct Investment (FDI) rather than Foreign Institutional Investment (FII) in India, in as much as empirical studies of the effects of FDI have reached more definitive conclusions than those on purely financial flows. The relation between growth and FDI is more prominent than that of between growth and portfolio capital flows. After more than decade of reforms, some fiscal indicators are in favour to India, reflecting a much more comfortable fiscal situation now, as compared to the crisis. This is reflected in less liquidity risk, lower external debt (most external debts are long-term in nature rather than short-term). Public debts are mostly local currency denominated and held by local residents.

However, there are some factors to which the country needs to be aware of. Though public debt is held by mostly domestic residents, it is much higher as a percentage of GDP compared to other similar credit-rating countries. The fiscal and primary deficits are also higher compared to other credit-rating countries. Public debt to revenue ratio (which is a better measure of sustainability compared to other indicators) is also much high. Though there is less probability of a decline in revenue, the revenue is not increasing over time.

High percentage of government debt is held by commercial banks. This adversely affected the capital adequacy ratio of the banks. Though there is no potential fear of external crisis due to much less external debt, the situation may be vulnerable to an internal crisis on the absence of transparency and significant reduction in NPAs. Since Government is not supposed to default on her debt obligations, the rising internal public debt is not taken care of, and capital is not allocated to pre-empt any future losses. Moreover, if depositors became suspicious about the quality of government debt there is a potential fear of bank run, and implicit losses may turn to be actual.

Therefore, some policy options which needs to be taken care of before approaching towards full CAC (or which can be undertaken simultaneously with CAC in a phased manner) are—

- Greater thrust and diversification of the export sector.
- Greater thrust to negotiations on bilateral or regional trading agreements (RTAs), especially with SAARC countries, particularly with Bangladesh, Bhutan, Sri Lanka, Thailand, China and MERCOSUR. While maintaining the current trading patterns with the developed countries and gradually shifting through RTAs with the developing economies, India can improve her position in merchandise trade. Many less developing countries (LDCs) produce necessary industrial intermediate inputs, which are often used by India. Most of these countries are not a direct competitor of India in the international market. Therefore, greater benefit can be realized through RTAs with these countries.
- Processing facilities in the export sector are to be improved. Improvements are also needed in basic infrastructure like storage and transportation.
- Greater concentration is to be placed on infrastructure.
- Reduction in variations of FDI in States by making less FDI recipient States more reform-oriented.
- Greater incentives should be placed on servicing

related to medical transcriptions, content development and pharmaceutical industries.

- Selective withdrawals of caps on FDI in information technology (IT) and drugs sector.
- Greater importance in exchange rate management by suitable monetary policies.
- Increasing incentives to the exporters of manufacturing items and attention is to be given for the improvement of Export Processing Zones. (EPZs)
- It should be remembered that lower debt-service payments is due to the reduced debt burden and also due to huge non-debt creating inflows like FIIs. The stability of this source in the long-run is yet to be justified.
- Though NRI seems to be a stable source of inflows, it depends on standard risk and return. Therefore, sound macroeconomic policies are to be maintained.

Notes and References

1. Some economists opine that rupee appreciation has, in fact, some beneficial impact on domestic exporters, as this leads to a substantial decline in the cost of imported raw materials, which forms a significant proportion of exports. This is true in case of diamond, high-end textile and engineering industries. This helps domestic exporters in case of their cost-competitiveness.
2. Suppose e=50 Rs./dollar, which means one dollar can buy fifty rupees. If rupee appreciates against the dollar, say to e=40 Rs./dollar, then e declines, which means rupee becomes expensive relative to dollar.
3. Let $dp^*/p^*=0$. Then, $dR/R=de/e - dp/p$. Since $de/e<0$ and $dp/p>0$ for the Indian economy, $dR/R<0$.

References

Ahluwalia, Montek S. (2002): "India's Vulnerability to External Crisis: An Assessment", in *Macroeconomic and Monetary Policy: Issues for Reforming the Economy*, edited by Montek AhJuwalia, S.S. Tarapore and Y.V. Reddy, New Delhi: Oxford University Press.

Arteta, Carlos, Barry Eichengreen and Charles Wyplosz (2001): "When Does Capital Account Liberalization Help More Than It hurts?", *NBER Working Paper*, 8414.

Chaudhuri, Tamal Dutta (2006): 'Capital Account Convertibility, the South Asian Crisis and their Implications with Respect to the Indian Economy', in *Financial Sector Reforms* published by ICFAI University Press.

Dondapath, Aruna Kumar (2006): "Participatory Notes: Boon or Bane?", in *Financial Markets, Corporate Restructuring*, ICFAI READER, ICFAI University Press.

Ghosh, Arunava (2004): "India's Pathway Through Financial Crisis", *Global Economic Governance Working Paper*, 2004/06, Department of Politics and International Relations, Oxford University College.

Gordon, James and Gupta Poonam (2004): "Non-resident Deposits in India: In Search of Return?" Asia and Pacific Department, *IMF Working Paper* WP/04/48, International Monetary Fund.

Government of India, *Economic Survey*, various years, New Delhi: Ministry of Finance.

Gupta, Poonam: "Macroeconomic Determinants of Remittances: Evidences from India", *IMF Working Paper*/05/224, December 2005, p. 8.

Henry, Peter (2003): "Capital Account Liberalization, the Cost of Capital and Economic Growth", *NBER Working Paper*.

Jadav, Narendra: "Capital Account Liberalizations: The Indian Experience" Paper presented at the Conference on 'A Tale of Two Giants: India's and China's Experience with Reform and Growth', New Delhi, November, 2003.

Karmakar, Asim K. (2007): "India's Foreign Exchange Reserves: A Synoptic Review", *Rabindra Bharati Journal of Economics*, March 2007, Vol. 1.

Kletzer, Kenneth M. (2004): "Liberalizing Capital Flows in India: Financial Repression, Macroeconomic Policy and Gradual Reforms." Santa Cruz Center for International Economics, *Working Paper* Series 1039, Center for International Economics UC Santa Cruz.

Krueger, Anne (1998): "Implications of the Asian Currency Crisis and the Debt Crisis of the 1980s," *Occasional Paper*, No. 3, University of Tasmania.

Mohan, Rakesh (2002): "Transforming Indian Banking: In Search of a Better Tomorrow." Speech delivered on December 29, Mumbai, India: Reserve Bank of India.

Patnaik, Ila and Ajay Shah (2004): "Interest Rate Volatility and Risk in Indian Banking." *Working Paper*, 04/17. International Monetary Fund.

Raju, M.T. and Anirban Ghosh (2004): "Market Volatility- An International Comparison", *Working Paper* series No. 8, Securities and Exchange Board of India.

Ramkishen S. Rajan and Rahul Sen (2002): "A Decade of Trade Reforms in India—it Compares with East Asia," Vol. 3, No. 4, *World Economics*,

Reserve Bank of India: *Handbook of Statistics of the Indian Economy*, Various issues.

Roubini, Nouriel and Richard Hemming (2004): 'A Balance Sheet Crisis in India?' Paper presented at the IMF/NIPFP Conference on Fiscal Policy in India, Taj Mahal Hotel, New Delhi, India, January 16-17, 2004.

Sen, Partha (2006): 'Case Against Rushing Towards Full Capital Account Convertibility', *EPW*,

Sur, Debashis and Joydeep Biswas (2006): "Effect of Institutional Investments on the Indian Stock Market", Research Paper, in *ICFAI READER Corporate Restructuring*, ICFAI University Press.

10

Capital Account Convertibility and Foreign Exchange Reserves in the Context of Asian Economies

PUSHPA TARAFDAR

ABSTRACT

Over the last few years economists have started referring to the substantial accumulation of foreign exchange reserves and growing current account surplus in a number of Asian countries. Many East Asian countries are accumulating dollar assets as a by-product of a strategy of export-led growth. The accumulation of reserves has been particularly significant in China, India, Japan, Korea, Pakistan and Taiwan.

In the above context, the paper examines the issue of capital account liberalization and convertibility in India. It also deals with the behaviour of capital flows in the 1990s and its impact on exchange rate movement.

The robust volume of capital flows to emerging markets reflects ample global liquidity, low interest rates in mature markets and successful reforms in most emerging countries. The behaviour of capital flows during 1990s in the emerging economies reveals that these flows can increase rapidly but can be highly volatile. Emerging market economies, thus, need to be equipped to deal with such volatility in order to ensure monetary and financial stability. Notwithstanding, the recovery in capital flows, emerging market economies, as a group, have become net exporters of capital to the mature economies since 2000. Three key factors explain the recent movement in capital flows. First, EMEs have recorded current account surpluses. The emergence of surpluses reflects the adjustment process in response to the financial crisis in Asia and elsewhere. Second, global imbalances, a large US current account deficit also explains the reverse capital movements for EMEs. Third, the movements in capital flows reflect the accumulation of reserves to maintain a competitive exchange rate. Reflecting all these factors, foreign exchange reserves of the developing countries increased by US Dollar 1256 billion between 1996 and 2004.

Most economies in Asia underwent capital account liberalization since 1980s. This liberalization trend was largely driven by globalization of financial flows. While opening up of the capital account may be conducive to economic growth, actual performance of the economy, however, typically depends on a host of other factors including sound macroeconomic policies and strong domestic financial system.

In India, the move towards full capital account liberalization has been approached with extreme caution. Reversal of the process of capital account liberalization can be prevented if reforms are appropriately sequenced. Capital account liberalization should be preceded by macroeconomic stabilization.

SECTION I

INTRODUCTION

Over the last few years economists have started referring to the substantial accumulation of international reserves and growing current account surplus in a number of Asian Countries. Many East Asian countries are accumulating dollar assets as a by-product of a strategy of export-led growth. The stock of foreign exchange assets exceeded $ 1,800 billion ($ 1,200 billion excluding Japan) at end of 2003, equal to half the global reserves. Asian Central Banks used the reserves to finance well over half of the current account deficit and budget deficit of the United Sates.

However, the amount of reserves appears to be more than what would be warranted by economic fundamentals (*IMF,* 2003). The accumulation has been particularly significant in Peoples' Republic of China (PRC), India, Japan, Korea, Pakistan and Taipei, China where growth rate of reserves has exceeded 20 percent during the last 2 years. In this respect worth mention are the PRC and India, which recorded average growth rates of about 30 percent in 2001-03.

In the above context, the paper examines the issue of capital account liberalization and convertibility in India. Section II is devoted to analyze the behaviour of capital flows and the exchange rate movement in the 1990s. Section III offers a broad review of the policy of capital account convertibility adopted in India. The final section offers a few concluding remarks.

SECTION II

As a part of the reform process, widespread and extensive reforms in the external sector have transformed India from a relatively closed economy to a fairly open economy. In the external sector, as in other areas, India has followed a cautious approach to capital account convertibility, exchange rate management, and trade liberalization. Careful monitoring of capital account transactions has been advocated to ensure an orderly process of liberalization and macroeconomic stability with a view to sustainability of the balance of payments and overall macroeconomic stability.

As regards capital flows, although the period since 1993-94 has been largely marked by persistent surpluses in the balance of payments, the period also witnessed a number of shocks such as the Asian financial crisis, sanctions resulting from the nuclear explosions, credit rating downgrades and the bursting of the information technology bubble in the U.S. These episodes have had repercussions on capital flows and exchange rates. Swing in capital flows, exchange rates and external demand conditions affect not only output and inflation, but also have impact upon banking and financial stability. More recently, the unprecedented volume of capital flows during 2003-04 threw new challenge for the conduct of monetary policy. Since 1991, there has been a continuous move towards integration of the Indian economy with the world economy. During this continuation of reforms four distinct phases are clearly discernible in terms of the underlying balance of payments conditions, shifts in monetary conditions and the policy response.

The first phase—the period 1993-95 was characterized by strong capital inflows accompanied with stability in the exchange rates. During this period, foreign investment inflows—in particular, portfolio investments inflows in the form of foreign institutional investors (FII) inflows and global depository receipt (GDR) increased sharply. Net portfolio inflows increased from negligible level to more than US $ 3 billion in each of the few years. Coupled with curtailment of the current account deficit there were large overall surpluses in the balance of payments and this led to a significant increase in foreign exchange reserves from their extremely low levels of the crisis period. During this period, the rupee witnessed a remarkable stability *vis-à-vis* the U.S. dollar.

The second phase - the year 1995-96 was characterized by a deceleration in capital flows and a widening of the current account deficit. There was a turnaround in the foreign exchange market and the prolonged stability in the exchange rate of the rupee witnessed from March 1993 came under stress in the second half of the 1995-96. In response to the upheavals, the Reserve Bank of India intervened in the market to signal that the fundamentals were in place and ensured that market corrections of the overvalued exchange rate was orderly and calibrated.

The third phase—1996-2001 witnessed return of capital inflows. This phase was marked with heightened volatility in capital flows. The volatility was on account both international and domestic factors—the Asian financial crisis, the spread of contagion to other markets such as Russia and Brazil, border tensions and sanctions imposed after nuclear tests. This necessitated policy initiatives to manage volatility in capital flows, including monetary measures, sales of foreign currency in the market to meet temporary demand-supply mismatches and administrative measures. Notwithstanding brief episodes of volatility, capital flows remained vastly in excess of current account deficits—which remained moderate in the face of low domestic absorption. As a result, the foreign exchange reserves increased on an average, by nearly U.S. $ 4.1 billion per year.

The fourth phase 2001-02 onwards posed new challenges for the conduct of monetary policy. This period has been marked by sustained surges in capital inflows coupled with surpluses in current account in the balance of payments. On the capital account, there was unprecedented volume of net inflows. With both current and capital account in surplus, foreign exchange markets were marked by persistent excess supply conditions. These excess supplies were absorbed by the Reserve Bank and as a result, its foreign exchange reserves more than doubled during the 3 year period from U.S. $ 42.3 billion at the end of March 2001 to U.S. $ 113.00 billion at the end of March 2004—an average increase of U.S. $ 23.6 billion per annum.

The Institute of International Finance (IIF) forecasts that net capital flows to emerging market economies are likely to grow to $ 225 billion in 2004 following a gain of over 50 percent to $ 194 billion in 2003. The robust volume of capital flows to emerging markets reflects ample global liquidity, low interest rates in mature markets, successful reforms in most emerging countries, and a progressive strengthening of activity in both industrial and emerging market economies. In particular, Asia continues to account for the largest part of FDI flows to emerging markets with PRC alone seeing FDI inflows of around $ 53 billion compared to about $ 49 billion in 2003. Nevertheless, countries like India, which has been increasingly receiving short-term portfolio flows, may be more concerned with outflows than others (Table 1).

The behaviour of capital flow during 1990s in the emerging market economies reveals that these flows can increase rapidly but can be highly volatile. Surges in capital flows and the associated volatility have implications for the conduct of monetary, exchange rate and the foreign exchange reserve policies. Emerging market economies, thus, need to be equipped to deal with such volatility in order to ensure monetary and financial stability. A striking feature of the last 3-4 years is two-way movement of capital between Emerging Market Economies (EMEs) and mature economies.

TABLE 1

Net Capital Flows to Emerging Markets

(US $ Billion)

Items	*1996*	*1997*	*1998*	*1999*	*2000*	*2001*	*2002*	*2003*
All EMEs Net inflows	74.4 (1.3)	47.3 (0.8)	104.2 (1.7)	5.2 (0.1)	-99.1 (-1.6)	-49.9 (-0.8)	-90.5 (-1.4)	-137.7 (-1.9)
Crisis Countries Net Inflows	53.6 (2.4)	64.8 (2.9)	18.7 (1.0)	-21.6 (-1.3)	-33.9 (-1.9)	-30.4 (-1.8)	-57.6 (-3.7)	-72.0 (-3.9)
Non-Crisis Countries Net Inflows	20.9 (0.6)	-17.5 (-0.4)	85.5 (2.1)	26.8 (0.6)	-65.2 (-1.4)	-19.5 (-0.4)	-32.8 (-0.7)	-65.8 (-1.2)

Source: *Global, Financial Stability Report IMF*, September 2004.

Notwithstanding the recovery in capital flows, emerging market economies, as a group, have become net exporters of capital to the matured economies since 2000. Two key factors explain the recent movement in capital flows (IMF 2004). First, EMEs have recorded current account surpluses. As against deficit of US $ 65 billion per annum during the 1990s, the emerging market economies recorded a surplus of US $ 149 billion during 2000-03. The emergence of surpluses reflected the adjustment process in response to the financial crisis in Asia and elsewhere. Countries that experienced crisis had to reduce domestic absorption and increase exports to generate a trade surplus. This process is quite high in East Asian Countries which have seen a sharp turnaround in their current accounts (Table 2).

Countries affected by crisis were also forced external deleveraging, i.e., a reduction in their external liabilities which also explain the pattern of capital outflows since 2001. A large US current account deficit also explains the reverse capital movements from EMEs.

The need for reserves as self-insurance emanates from the volatile nature of the capital flows. It also reflects weakness in the existing financial architecture. Capital flows have been observed to reverse quickly, leaving the country exposed to liquidity crisis.

As IMF (2003) finds, the level of reserve accumulation

TABLE: 2

Current Account Bahaviour in Select Economies Percentage of GDP

Country	*1991-96*	*1998-2003*
China	0.9	2.4
India	-1.1	-0.1
Indonesia	-1.3	0.5
Korea	-2.3	3.1
Malaysia	-6.4	11.4
Philippines	-3.8	4.6
Thailand	-6.4	8.1
Mexico	-4.2	-2.8

Source: International Economic Trends, Federal Reserve Bank of St. Louis, July 2004 as represented in Report on Currency and Finance, 2003-04.

TABLE 3

Total Reserves Accumulation

(US $ Billion)

Area/Country	*December 1996*	*December 2003*	*June 2004*	*Variance*[a]
All Counties	1647	3156	3463	1816
Industrial Countries	789	1219	1349	560
Japan	217	663	808	591
Developing Countries	858	1938	2114	1256
Asia	495	1248	1385	890
China P.R. Mainland	107	408	475	368
Taiwan Prov of China	88	207	230	142
Korea	34	155	167	133
China P.R. Hongkong	64	118	121	57
India	20	99	115	95
Singapore	77	96	102	25
Malaysia	27	45	54	27

Note: (a) Variation between June 2004 and December 1996.

Source: International Financial Statistics, IMF.

in some of the Asia economies has become much higher than warranted by conventional determinants, such as economic size, level of imports, export volatility; and exchange rate flexibility (Table 3). Decomposing the change in reserves - reveals that 13 sample economies can be grouped into roughly three sub-groups that are experiencing: (i) current account surplus and net capital inflows, (ii) current account surplus and net capital outflows, and (iii) relatively small balance of payments activity (Table 4). All sample economies with the exception of Pakistan and Vietnam reported current account surplus as of end 2003. One notable observation, however, is a difference in the trade balance. In countries where service sector is strong (i.e. Hong Kong; China; India; Pakistan; Philippines), the current account surplus is supported by the service trade surplus, or more precisely, remittances from residents abroad, e.g. Philippines. (Table 4)

TABLE 4

Grouping by Current Account and Capital Account Positions

(As of end-2003)

Group A (5 Economies) Current Account Surplus and Capital Inflows	*Group B (5 Economies) Current Account Surplus and Capital Outflows*	*Group C (3 Economies) All Accounts Less than $ 5 billion*
PRC	Hong Kong, China	
India	Indonesia	Pakistan
Japan	Malaysia	Philippines
Korea	Singapore	Viet Nam
Taipei, China	Thailand	

Source: International Financial Statistics, IMF.

After a period of post-crisis drying up of capital inflows, capital flows turned around to an upward trend during the past few years driven by both "Push"—the recovery of the world economy and low rate of returns outside, and "pull" rapid economic growth of some countries. Inflows during the past few years, however, were concentrated in limited countries: PRC; India; Japan; Korea; and Taipei, China (group A) which attracted more capital than they export. The PRC is the leading capital importer (except for Japan), receiving $ 61 billion in 2003, largely as a pipeline commitments for new foreign investment, followed by $ 17 billion to Korea and $ 11 billion to India.

China was again the largest recipient of FDI, not only in the region but also among all developing countries worldwide. Strong economic growth, an improved policy environment and further opening up to FDI in certain industries—such as banking and other financial services—contributed to the increase. Investments by private equity and venture capital funds, specially from the United States, have become important sources of foreign investment in China.

Two major components of capital (or more precisely financial) flows are equity investment and commercial bank flows. The PRC has become by far the most attractive destination of equity investment, receiving about $ 190 billion during the past 4 years or about 4 percent of GDP on an average. On the other hand, portfolio investments to countries like Korea have recently significantly decreased from about $ 59 billion in the early 1990s to $ 14 billion accounting for a share of only 5 percent of the total flow to the sample countries. There was sharp rise in net portfolio capital inflows specially into PRC, India, and Japan as well as Taipei China. In India, portfolio flows (1.7 percent of GDP) have become more prominent exceeding the direct investment (0.8 percent of GDP) in 2003. For the PRC direct investment (3.5 percent of GDP) is still the major part of equity investment. (Table 5)

The trend of commercial bank flows is distinct from that of equity investment. The dramatic change is found around the time of the Asian Financial crisis in 1997. The contagious withdrawal of capital from the region—sudden stop of capital inflows—forces the crisis hit countries to suffer from liquidity crunches. Three crisis-hit countries, Indonesia, Philippines and Thailand, still experienced net outflows in 2003. There are only three countries that attracted sizeable bank inflows—PRC, India and Korea. They attracted about $4 billion (India), $5 billion (PRC), and $10 billion (Korea) in 2003 while Malaysia and Viet Nam received less than a billion.

TABLE 5

Net FDI and Portfolio Investment

(Millions of US$)

	Cumulative Flows (1993-96)	*Share of Total Flows (Percent)*	*Cumulative Flows (2000-03)*	*Share of Total Flows (Percent)*
PRC	132.753	47	187.600	71
India	19.707	7	30.779	12
Korea	58.745	21	13.546	5
Indonesia	14.636	5	10.715	4
Thailand	10.186	4	1.473	4
Malaysia	29.243	10	4.358	2
Philippines	8.204	3	3.757	1
Vietnam	3.226	1	2.260	1
Pakistan	4.473	2	2.042	1
Total	281.173	100	265.530	100

Source: Institute of International Finance.

Volatility of the capital account may vary due to the different types of flows they are experiencing. Past studies show that FDI tends to be least volatile, while portfolio and bank flows tend to be more volatile. Countries like India, where portfolio and bank flows are more significant than FDI, appear most fragile to capital account development, while it is less so in the PRC. Nevertheless, the volatility and actual magnitude of outflows, are significantly affected by the extent of capital controls that each country adopts.

South-East Asia witnessed rise in capital inflows from $17 billion in 2003 to $26 billion in 2004. Higher capital inflows to Singapore, Malaysia, Indonesia, Myanmar, Viet Nam, the Philippines, and Cambodia contributed to the region's increased FDI receipts.

The rapid rise of FDI inflows to the region and the narrowing gap between flows to ASEAN members and China assuaged those concerned that China is crowding out FDI from its neighbouring countries. A recent study suggests that

FDI in China did not crowd out FDI inflows in South Asian countries during 1992-2001. This is based on the fact that export-oriented FDI in China may have been so far complementary to that in South-East Asian countries.

In view of improved economic situation in the region, a better policy environment, and significant regional integration efforts, the prospects for FDI flows to Asia and Oceania are highly positive. The recent increase in cross-border M & As in countries such as China, India and the Republic of Korea supports this optimistic assessment of FDI prospects in the region. However, flows are likely to remain concentrated in a few economies.

Most economies in Asia underwent capital account liberalization starting in the mid-1980s. This liberalization trend was largely driven by the globalization of financial flows. As stated earlier the trend resulted in massive capital outflows during the Asian financial crisis and sudden stop of capital inflows. Consequently, a few countries (Indonesia, Malaysia and Philippines) reversed this liberalization trend and the capital account are currently only partially liberalized. Conversely, economies such as Hong Kong, China, Japan, Korea, Taipei, China and Thailand have continued with liberalization of their capital accounts till now.

Alternatively, countries that were not directly affected by the Asian crisis, such as the PRC, India, Pakistan and Vietnam, for example, still maintain capital controls in almost all area. In India, liberalization has mainly focused on direct and portfolio investments by non-residents starting in 1991. In these areas, free entry and exit is now the normal rule. Significant casing has taken Place in January 2004, the RBI abolished capital-size restrictions on overseas investments by Indian companies and eased discretionary rules on external commercial borrowings. Further, controls on personal transfers abroad up to $ 25,000 have been lifted recently. However, debt-creating external borrowings is flightily controlled, particularly, if short-term. Also banks and money markets generally face significant restrictions on their foreign operations as capital outflows by residents continue to be strictly forbidden. For the PRC, inward FDI was the first to be liberalized in the early 1990s. However, the liberalization of capital restrictions on other areas has been very little, and flows are still tightly restricted and need layers of permissions.

In India, the experience with liberalization of inward capital flows had been similar to the economies of Latin America and crisis-hit Asia and only the magnitude of these flows has not been larger enough to cause serious macro and micro-management problems.

The net capital inflows reached 8-9 percent of GDP in 1996 in the crisis hit economies as opposed to only 1.9 percent in India in 2003.

Nevertheless, the Indian Government has taken steps to liberalize outflows of capital in 2004. But this is perhaps a risky proposition. The embrace of full convertibility is itself likely to bring more dollars into the country in the initial phase and add to the existing upward pressure on the rupee. In fact, strong economic growth, continuing low interest rates and the strong performance of the equity market suggest that reduction in payments restrictions have not significantly dampened reserve growth.

In sum, risks of capital flight are limited so long as capital controls stay in place. Nevertheless, further loosening of controls in capital outflows, combined with the past evidence of ineffective capital controls in some countries poses a risk of outflows. There are also external factors. As recovery in mature markets emerges and liquidity surge in Asia drives down domestic interest rates, the interest rate differentials would narrow further, which would certainly work as a pull factor out of emerging markets.

Section III

With the growing role of private capital flows and the possibility of occasional sharp reversals, issue of capital account liberalization has spurred extensive debate since 1992—the period which witnessed a series of currency crisis. In Europe (1992-93), Mexico (1994-95), East Asia (1997-98),Brazil (1999) and Argentina (2001-02). These crises have raised the question of desirability of liberalization and whether it is advisable to vest the IMF with the responsibility for promoting the orderly liberalization of capital flows. The IMF in its study (1998) stated that as liberalized systems afford opportunities for individual, enterprises and financial institutions to undertake greater and sometimes imprudent risks, they create the potential for systematic disturbances. There is no way to completely suppress these dangers other-than-through draconian financial repression, which is more damaging. The view of IMF itself has changed overtime (*RBI*, 2001). While opening up of the capital account may be conducive to economic growth as it could make available larger stock of capital for a capital-deficient country, the actual performance of the economy, however, typically depends on a host of other factors. For a successful liberalized capital account, emerging market countries should: (i) pursue sound macroeconomic policies, (ii) strengthen the domestic financial, (iii) phase capital account liberalization appropriately, and (iv) provide information to the market. At the international level, there is also the role of surveillance to consider, including the provision of information and the potential need for financing.

In India, the move towards full capital account liberalization has been approached with extreme caution. The Report of the Committee on Capital Account Convertibility (Chairman S.S. Tarapore) taking into account lessons from international experiences suggested a number of signposts, the attainment of which are a necessary concomitant in the move towards capital account convertibility. Fiscal consolidation, lower inflation and a stronger financial system were seen as crucial signposts in India.

Recommendation for Capital Account convertibility by Tarapore Committee were the following:

Fiscal Consolidation

(1) Reduction in gross fiscal deficit as percentage of gross domestic product from budgeted 4.5 percent in 1997-98 to 4.0 in 1998-99 and further to 3.5 in 1999-2000.

Mandated Inflation Rate

(1) The mandated rate of inflation for the three year period from 1997-98 to 1999-2000 should be an average of 3 to 5 percent.

(2) The Reserve Bank should be given the freedom to attain mandated rate of inflation approved by the Parliament.

Strengthening Financial System

(1) Interest rates should be fully deregulated in 1997-98 and any formal or informal interest rate controls to be abolished.

(2) CRR to be reduced in phases to 8 percent in 1997-98, 6 percent in 1998-99 and to 3% 1999-2000.

Gross Non- performing Assets (NPAs) as percentage of total advances to be brought down in phases to 12 percent in 1997-98 to 9 percent in 1998-99 and to 5 percent 1999-2000.

100 percent marketed to market valuation of investments for banks.

Best practices for forex risk management by banks:

Important Macroeconomic Indicators

1. A monitoring band of +/- 5 percent around the neutral Real Effective Exchange Rate (REER) to be introduced and intervened by the Reserve Bank when REER is outside the band.
2. Debt-service ratio to be reduced to 20 percent from 25 percent.
3. The foreign exchange reserves should not be less than 6 months imports.

Developments

1. Gross Fiscal Deficit as a percentage of gross domestic product stood at 5.9 during 2002-03,
2. Annual inflation rate based on WPI (base 1993-94

= 100) averaged at 4.7 percent during the three years period 1999-2000 to 2001-02.

3. All interest rates have been deregulated.
4. CRR reduced to 4.75 percent in 2002-03.

Capital Account Liberalization and its Reversal—Cross Country Experience

A number of southern cone countries in Latin America undertook rapid liberalization of their capital account in the late 1970s in conjunction with a pre-announced or fixed exchange rate. Asian countries, such as Malaysia, Indonesia and Singapore also liberalized their capital account against the background of strong balance of payments position. Many countries prematurely opened their capital account. There was a reversal in the process of liberalization among many developing countries in the early 1980s. Pre-existing weaknesses in the banking system led to the emergence of serious banking problems which in turn led to the re-imposition of controls in Southern cone countries and debt crisis-led countries in Latin America.

The process of capital account opening in developing countries accelerated in the 1990s, especially with emerging market economies substantially liberalizing their capital controls in Asia, Latin America and transition economies. Argentina had to re-impose controls in its capital account in December 2001 in the wake of unprecedented sovereign debt crisis. In the aftermath of the Asian crisis of 1997, the international perception on liberalization of capital accounts and the national policy thinking on the relative benefits of an open capital account *vis-à-vis* the associated costs have changed considerably. The policy debate now centres around the contours of an orderly liberalization framework and countries like Malaysia have even reverted to capital controls as the key instrument of crisis management.

Reversal of the process of capital account liberalization can be prevented if reforms are appropriately sequenced. Appropriate sequencing of capital flow depends on the initial conditions. It is generally agreed that capital account liberalization should be preceded by macroeconomic stabilization.

In general, liberalization of the capital account should follow the current account since the former may involve real appreciation of the exchange rate whereas the latter may require a real depreciation to offset the adverse impact of the dismantling of tariff and non-tariff protection on the balance of payments. Reform of the domestic financial markets before capital account liberalization is generally considered critical; since domestic financial institutions can then be better equipped to face international competition and to intermediate movement of funds efficiently without exposing the system to unavoidable risks.

Unless banking standards are accordingly improved, viable competition introduced, and government interference reduced, it would be reckless to pursue full capital account convertibility, which requires flexibility, dynamism, and foresight in the country's banking and financial institutions. The increasing contribution of portfolio capital toward the capital account and the fact that these inflows could increase to significant levels in the future as financial markets get integrated globally, their skillful management is an important condition to facilitate smooth intermediation. Banks intermediate a substantial amount of funds, e.g. over 64 percent of total financial assets in India.

Discipline in Fiscal and Financial Policies

It is well known that to gain confidence of investors it is necessary for the Government follow prudent fiscal policy. Asian countries have been relatively prudent in Government spending except India. In India, the ratio of gross fiscal deficit to GDP increased to 11 percent in 2003 from 6.2 percent in 1996-97. Such high fiscal deficits can prove to be highly unsustainable and can frighten investors away. Hence, there is an immediate need for putting brakes on Government expenditure, and until that has not been successfully done, opening up the capital account fully would carry with it a big risk of sudden loss of faith of investors as well as capital flight.

The impact of the continuous reforms initiated since 1991 resulted in an accumulation of foreign exchange reserves of over US $ 70 billion at end-February 2003. Capital account surplus increased from US $ 3.9 billion during the 1980s to US $ 8.6 billion during 1992-2002 with a steadily rising foreign investment. As a proportion of GDP, capital flows increased from 1.6 percent during 1980s to 2.3 percent during 1992-2002. The significant increase in capital flows during the 1990s raises the issue for their determinants as well as their impact on growth. Granger causality test indicate a unidirectional causation from net capital flows to growth in GDP over the 1970-2000 period. Apart from financing current account gap, capital flows have played a significant role in India's growth performance.

References

Agarwala, Ramgopal (2003-04): "Towards a Multipolar World of International Finance," *Indian Economic Journal*, July-Sept. 2003-04.

Akiko Terada, Hagiwara (2005): "Foreign Exchange Reserves, Exchange Rate and Monetary Policy: Issues in Asia," *Asian Development Review*, Vol. 22, No. 2, pp. 2, 6-8, 26-28.

International Monetary Fund (2003): *World Economic Outlook*, Washington DC

Reserve Bank of India: *Report on Currency and Finance, 2001-02, 2003-04*.

Tarafdar, Puspa (2000): "Exchange Rate Behaviour in Developing Countries in Context of India" in Alak Ghosh and Rakesh Raman (eds.), *Exchange Rate Behaviour in Developing Countries*, pp. 143-48, Deep & Deep Publications Pvt. Ltd., New Delhi.

United Nations Conference on Trade and Development, 2005.

World Investment Report, 2002, 2005,

11

Asset Price Volatility and Capital Account Liberalization: A Rational Expectation Model

SAIKAT BHATTACHARYYA

ABSTRACT

Financial Globalization is the imperative of time. This paper seeks to find out, in light of Rational Expectation Hypothesis, whether it has any impact on stock price volatility. Rational expectation-based dividend discount model of asset price determination is used here and solved through recursive method to have multiple equilibria. One of the solutions leads the stock price to be equal to present value of future flow of dividends, the true value of the asset. All other solutions imply the existence of rational bubble. Whatever may be the case, we find if the dividend from a domestic stock follows a well-defined path with random fluctuation (which follows first-order auto-regression AR[1]) around it, any process of liberalization, which also has its own path with white noise disturbances, is not going to inject any additional volatility in stock prices, provided the agents behaves rationally using all the information they have under a perfect information assumption.

Acknowledgement: *Support and helpful comments on earlier drafts from Dr. Ratan Kumar Ghosal, Professor in Economics, Department of Commerce. University of Calcutta and Mr. Aniruddha Mitra, Ph.D. student, Department of Economics, University of Illinois at Urbana-Campaign; are gratefully acknowledged.*

I. INTRODUCTION

Since early 1990s, inflow of private capital into the emerging market economies has increased significantly. This is mostly due to the fact that these emerging economies have made their financial sector open for foreign capital. Henry (1997b) analyzes a group of 11 countries and shows empirically that stock market liberalization has a positive impact on the private investment. Assets of these countries have become more attractive and inflow of foreign fund is raising the price of the equities. Henry (1997a) shows how the equity prices have increased. Now the question is whether the liberalization of financial market has increased the volatility of the stock (here we'll use the terms stock, share, equity synonymously) market compared to the pre-liberalization era. In this epoch of globalization, capital is moving freely across the globe. All types global portfolio fund is venturing around the world for speculative gain. Conventional wisdom suggests that this will enhance the volatility of stock price. Hence, to resist this instability some sort of restrictions are required to protect free flow of hot money. There are theoretical literatures supporting this conventional wisdom. Erturk (2005) outlined a 'non-imperfectionist' account of why and how the capital account liberalization can systematically lead to economic volatility even in the absence of market imperfection. He has pointed out that opening up of the capital account opens the scope for currency substitution and erratic capital movements across the border. These two factors are intertwined with each other and make the asset price more volatile. Bacchetta and Wincoop (1998) analyze the impact of financial liberalizations and reforms in emerging markets on the dynamics of these markets. They show that liberalization leads to rich dynamics of capital flows and often implies an

effect of random fluctuation of the dividend on the price of the stock. Whenever the economy is in depression we can expect a negative u_t and *vice versa.* It would not be very illogical to expect this random component fluctuates with the ups and downs of the business cycle. The third term shows the present value of the stream of successive 'tax' relives that one overseas investor expects, thanks to the liberalization programme. As we have assumed that the liberalization programme starts and terminates at period-0 and period-T respectively, total expected reduction of the value of the share would be $R\rho^t\tau_0 \frac{[1-(R\rho)^T]}{1-R\rho}$. Surely, this would be lower than the one with a constant high level of 'tax' (i.e. in a closed economy where $\tau_0 = \tau_1 = ...$). Symbolically,

$$R\rho^t\tau_0 \frac{[1-(R\rho)^T]}{1-R\rho} < R\tau_0 \frac{1-(R)^T}{1-R}$$

Thus liberalization raises the net present value of the future flow of earning of the asset. Hence, the domestic stock becomes more attractive to a foreign investor. These three components together constitute the net (net of tax) true present value of the share in addition to the random component. That is,

$$P_t^* = \frac{Ra(1+\gamma)^t}{1-R(1+\gamma)} - R\rho^t\tau_0 \frac{[1-(R\rho)^T]}{1-R\rho} + Ru_t \frac{1}{1-R\theta}.$$

The price of the share is supposed to be equal to this true present value plus the random component.

Case I (Solution without bubble)

Now imposing the *transversality condition,* i.e. $\lim_{i\to\infty} R^i E_t P_{t+1+i} = 0$, we have $P_t = P^*$. The presence of *transversality condition* rules out the possibility of a bubble. The restriction that is imposed on R (i.e. 0<R<1) is due to the presence of the arbitrage opportunity (see: Appendix: I) which ensures the equality between expected rate of return from (risky) stock market and the sum of risk free interest rate and the risk premium (risk premium is 0 for a neutral agent).

In absence of the bubble component what determines the variability of stock prices? When the dividend, the 'tax' component follows a known path with a pre-determined present value, the only variability determining factor happens to be the random term u_t. Surely,

$$Var(P^*) = \frac{R}{1-R\theta} Var(u_t) = \frac{R}{(1-R\theta)} \frac{\sigma^2}{(1-\theta^2)}$$

[Substituting the value of $Var(u_t)$].

The variability of the stock price depends on the variability of the random term. No 'tax' component is there. Hence, there is no impact of liberalization on the stock price volatility under perfect information and rational expectation.

Case II (Solution with bubble)

But this is one of the solutions. With the presence of the bubble, which is a non-stationary (i.e. relaxing the assumption of presence of arbitrage opportunity) we can expect multiple equilibria.

$$\text{Let } P_t = P_t^* + B_t \qquad (6)$$

where B_t is the bubble. The first term in equation 5, being the unexplained component with no base, is said to be the bubble.

Equation (6) to be a solution to the following condition has to be held (see Appendix III)

$$B_t = RE_tB_{t+1}$$

$$\text{or, } E_tB_{t+1} = R^{-1}B_t \Rightarrow E_tB_{t+i} = R^{-i}B_t \qquad (7)$$

Let the probability of a bubble to burst in each period is π (assumed to be exogenous). So, from equation (7) the value of the bubble at period (t+i) becomes

$$\left.\begin{aligned} B_{t+i} &= [R(1-\pi)]^{-i} B_t + e^3_{t+i} \text{ [probability } (1-\pi)] \\ B_{t+i} &= e^3_{t+i} \qquad\qquad\qquad \text{[probability } (\pi)] \end{aligned}\right\} \quad (8)$$

Now incorporating the above relationships and [assuming $E(e^3_{t+i}) = 0$] in equation (6) we have two alternative solutions for P_t, depending on whether the bubble bursts or not.

$$\left.\begin{aligned} P_t &= \lim_{i\to\infty}[R(1-\pi)]^{-i} B_0 + \frac{Ra(1+\gamma)^t}{1-R(1+\gamma)} - R\rho^t \tau_0 \frac{[1-(R\rho)^T]}{1-R\rho} + Ru_t \frac{1}{1-R\theta} \\ P_t &= \frac{Ra(1+\gamma)^t}{1-R(1+\gamma)} - R\rho^t \tau_0 \frac{[1-(R\rho)^T]}{1-R\rho} + Ru_t \frac{1}{1-R\theta} \end{aligned}\right\} \quad (9)$$

Whenever the bubbles are created and when it rises it continues to rise monotonically until it bursts and when it falls, it falls monotonically, and even it may be negative. A negative bubble may be ruled out, as it is unrealistic, but we can sensibly assume a secular downturn and let its lower limit be 0. This implies, whenever a bubble bursts the stock price takes its second alternative in equation (9) and if it grows it can grow limitlessly, as shown in the first alternative in equation (9). Whenever the bubble bursts the asset price becomes equal to P*. If the bubble bursts when $Ru_t \frac{1}{1-R\theta} \geq 0$, that is, when the economy is in upswing, P_t will continue to grow after a sudden fall and another bubble will be created. On the contrary if it bursts when $Ru_t \frac{1}{1-R\theta} < 0$, it will take the path of P* and move accordingly, as we have ruled out the possibility of a negative bubble. Thus if we accept the presence of a speculative bubble, erratic fluctuation in asset price is primarily determined by the bubble component and the probability of bursting becomes very important, as far as the volatility of the market is concerned. The bubble part does not include any tax component. Secondly, the random term u_t in p* is another volatility determining factor like case I. This random component, as shown before (in case I) is independent of the policy of globalization. So, the proposition, which follows from our model can be stated as: *if the dividend from a domestic stock follows a well-defined path with random fluctuation (which follows first-order autoregression AR[1]) around it, any process of liberalization, which also has its own path with white noise disturbances, is not going to inject any additional volatility in stock prices, provided the agents behaves rationally using all the information they have under a perfect information assumption, irrespective of existence of any speculative bubble.*

If the agents have all necessary information which plays any role in the determination of stock price, they can calculate the present value of the future flow of earning and can rationally anticipate the stock price. That is they have the idea of equation (5). So, whatever variability is there is due to the random component in the dividend path. If the policy change and its course are correctly anticipated by the agents there would not be any additional volatility. But if the policy-makers keep the agents in dark, though there is no plausible reason for doing it when the government has incentive to remain transparent, there might be some impact on volatility.

III. POLICY MATTERS

What we find in the earlier section that if the agents behave rationally, using all the available information the liberalization is not going to affect the variability of the asset price. Two components that we find in the earlier section, determine the volatility are the random term associated with the dividend path and the second one, perhaps the most important one, if it exists, is the bubble. These two components remain unaltered with any change in the policy of capital account liberalization. So, the volatility that was there will remain even after and during the process of liberalization. So, the role of government just becomes to pursue the capital account liberalization as decided and not to surprise the agents. That is, not to deviate too much from the 'tax' path.

Excessive erratic fluctuation in price of stock is not a very good sign as far as the domestic economy is concerned, as it introduces price risk and exposes the stock market to the speculators. With a fully convertible capital account with the scope of free inflow and outflow of global speculative funds may create the scope for capital flow reversal leaving the domestic economy in deep trouble. Hence, the government has a role to reduce the volatility of stock market. The objective of the policy should be to keep the price of the stock as close as possible to its true value. Transparency regarding business data and policy data is the prerequisite in this direction so that, the possibility of over expectation of asset prices becomes the least. Government should ensure that the business sector regularly publish data about their ongoing projects and the government should come clear about their short and long-run policy and let the people have the opportunity to acquire the required information before taking their decision. Secondly, the government should frame its policies to encourage the development of the risk minimizing financial instruments. That will directly and favourably attack the π component in equation (9). Mature and advance financial structure is the precondition for successful capital account liberalization. Some authors including Krugman (2000) and Stiglitz (2002) have argued that the financial markets of the emerging markets are poorly developed and thus they do not function properly like that of advanced countries. So before phasing out regulations on capital flow it requires to improve the financial structure by introducing necessary financial instruments. And while introducing the strategy, the government must be transparent and as well as be firm on the execution of the policy, so that no confusion arises among the agents.

IV. CONCLUDING REMARKS

Liberalization of capital account has become the imperative of time. It cannot be avoided. However, the policy-makers of the emerging countries are very skeptical as far as financial globalization is concerned. There are reasons to be so as it may instigate financial crisis, which may bring about a sudden reversal of capital, leaving the country in grave financial crisis. Instances of such financial crisis are not at all rare. The major concern of these policy-makers is that liberalization might inject additional volatility in the financial system of the country. Here, in light of rational expectation hypothesis we see that if information regarding the pace of liberalization is known to all the agents it cannot inject any additional volatility. Hence, the process of liberalization cannot be blamed for the erratic fluctuation and the resulting economic crisis. In fact, there are systemic or institutional errors in the underdeveloped financial structure of the emerging market economies, which should be corrected before phasing out restrictions on the flow of overseas capital.

Note

1. Blanchard Oliver Jean and Stanley Fischer (1989), "Multiple Equilibria, Bubbles, and Stability", chapter 5, pp. 213-74, *Lectures on Macroeconomic,* Prentice Hall of India Pvt. Ltd.—have showed a technique to solve the expectational difference equation. We have followed that methodology.

References

1. Bacchetta Philippe and Eric van Wincoop (1998); "Capital Flows to Emerging Markets: Liberalization, Overshooting and Volatility", *NBER Working Paper* No. 6530, April 1998.
2. Edwards, Sebastian, Javier Gomez Biscarri and Fernando Perez de Gracia (2003):"Stock Market Cycles, Financial Liberalization and Volatility", *NBER Working Paper* No 9817, July 2003.
3. Erturk, Korkut A. (2005): "Economic Volatility and Capital Account Liberalization in Emerging Countries"; *International Institute of Applied Economics,* Vol. 19, No. 4, October.
4. Henry, P.B. (1997a), "Stock Market Liberalization, Economic Reform, and Emerging Market Equity Price," *mimeo,* September.

5. Henry, P.B. (1997b); "Do Stock Market Liberalizations Cause Investment Booms?", *mimeo*, November.
6. Jayasuriya, Shamila (2005) "Stock market liberalization and volatility in the presence of favourable market characteristics and institutions"; *Emerging Markets Review*, Volume 6, Issue 2, June 2005, pp. 170-91.
7. Krugman, P. (2000): *The Return of Depression Economics*. Norton, New York.
8. LeRoy, Stephen, and Richard Porter. (1981): "The Present-Value Relation: Tests based on Implied Variance Bounds," *Econometrica*, 49 (May), pp. 555-74.
9. Shiller, Robert. (1981): "Do Stock Prices Move Too Much to be Justified by Subsequent Changes in Dividends?" *American Economic Review* 71 (June), pp. 421-36.
10. Stiglitz, J. (2002): *Globalization and its Discontents*, Norton, New York.
11. West, Kenneth. (1987): "A Specification Test for Speculative Bubbles," *The Quarterly Journal of Economics*, 102 (August), pp. 553-80.
12. West, Kenneth. (1988):"Dividend Innovations and Stock Price Volatility," *Econometrica*, 56 (January), pp. 37-61.

APPENDIX I

The (expected) rate of return of a unit of stock, purchased at the beginning of period t at price P_t and sold at the beginning of period t+1 at price P_{t+1} has two components: (1) the net (net of 'tax') dividend earned, and (2) the (expected) capital gain. This implies,

$$r = \frac{P_{t+1} - P_t}{P_t} + \frac{(d_t - \tau_t)}{P_t} \qquad (A.1)$$

$$\text{or, } P_t = \left[\frac{1}{1+r}\right][P_{t+1} + (d_t - \tau_t)]$$

Here, the expected rate of return, r is assumed to remain constant overtime. Even if we introduce fluctuating expected rate of return the main proposition of the model will remain unaltered. So, to avoid unnecessary computational complications r is supposed to be fixed here.

In presence of the possibility of *arbitrage,* r must be identical with the sum of risk free interest and risk premium.

Setting $R = \left[\frac{1}{1+r}\right]$ and introducing the expectation operator

we have $P_t = R[E_t P_{t+1} + (d_t - \tau_t)]$, which is equation (4).

APPENDIX II

Substituting the values of d_t, and τ_t from equation 1, 2 and 3 in equation 4 we have:

$$P_t = R[E_t P_{t+1} + a(1+\gamma)^t + u_t - \rho^t \tau_0 + e_t^2] \quad \text{(A.2)}$$

Pushing one period forward.

Taking expectation conditional on information at time t in both the sides of the equation

$$P_{t+1} = R[E_{t+1} P_{t+2} + a(1+\gamma)^{t+1} + u_{t+1} - \rho^{t+1} \tau_0 + e_{t+1}^2] \quad \text{(A.3)}$$

$\because E_t\{E_{t+1}P_{t+2}\} = E_t P_{t+2}$, which is due to *law of iterative expectation.* And as it is assumed earlier that $E(e_t^2) = 0$.

Substituting A.3 in A.2 we have

$$P_t = R^2 E_t P_{t+2} + Ra(1+\gamma)\{1 + R(1+\gamma)\} - R\rho^t \tau_0 (1 + R\rho) + R\{RE_t u_{t+1} + u_t\}$$

Extending in this way by repeated substitution,

$$P_t = \lim_{i\to\infty} R^i E_t P_{t+1+i} + Ra(1+\gamma)[1 + R(1+\gamma) + \{R(1+\gamma)\}^2 ....]$$
$$-R\rho^t \tau_0 [1 + (R\rho) + (R\rho)^2 + ...] + R\sum_{i=0}^{\infty} R^i E_t u_{t+i} \quad \text{(A.4)}$$

Equation 2 implies $u_{t+1} = \theta u_t + e_{t+1}^1$

Now taking expectation conditional on information at time t

$E_t u_{t+1} = \theta u_t$; By repeated substitution we have $E_t u_{t+i} = \theta^t u_t$. Substituting the value of $E_t u_{t+i}$ for each i=0, 1, 2, 3..........in A.4 we find equation 5.

APPENDIX: III

If $P_t = P_t^* + B_t$ then $E_t P_{t+1} = E_t P_{t+1}^* + E_t B_{t+1}$;

Replacing P_t and $E_t P_{t+1}$ in equation 4 we have:

$$P_t^* + B_t = R[E_t P_{t+1}^* + E_t B_{t+1} + (d_t - \tau_t)]$$

Hence, $B_t = R[E_t B_{t+1}]$ (A.5)

A.5 leads to equation 7.

Index